# Relocation 101
## Making the Most of Your Move

By
Beverly D. Roman

Copyright © 2007 BR Anchor Publishing. All rights reserved
Seventh Impression
Printed in Canada

All rights reserved. No part of this book may be reproduced or transmitted in any form or by any means, electronic or mechanical, including but not limited to photocopying, recording, or any information storage and retrieval system, without permission in writing from BR Anchor Publishing.

Published by BR Anchor Publishing

ISBN 1-888891-34-3

Edited by Dalene R. Bickel

Research and contributions by
Amy L. Roman, MA, Counseling/Psychology

Book design and layout by Michael J. Cadieux. Michael is an award-winning graphics designer and an accomplished illustrator. His creative art has graced all of BR Anchor Publishing's books.

Book cover is an original water color painting by Robert C. Arriola.

*Relocation 101* is distributed by:
BR Anchor Publishing
4596 Capital Dome Drive
Jacksonville, FL 32246-7457
In the United States: 1.800.735.9209
Tel: + 904.641.1140
Fax: + 904.641.1136
e-mail: aroman@branchor.com

Visit BR Anchor Publishing on the web: www.branchor.com for newsletter articles, book descriptions and more.
All books are described on page 124 in this book.

# PREFACE

My goal with my first book, *Moving Minus Mishaps*, was to share advice gathered through my own moving experiences. I believed the many tips I learned by trial and error could in turn benefit other families, saving them time, aggravation and money. As a stay-at-home mother, I took care of myriad details on my own, just a few of which included: smoothly transitioning children from school to school, buying a home in an appropriate community and often coping with medical emergencies before we were established with a local physician.

Even though relocation was certainly challenging 20 years ago, there are many more difficulties that need to be addressed in the 21st century. Today the majority of families are dual career couples with dependent children. In addition, the numbers of single parent families, male career-interrupted spouses, special needs workers and elder care responsibilities are increasing. All of these factors require specific relocation advice and services.

In *Relocation 101*, you will find "tried and true" advice based on my philosophy about moving: every relocation should become an opportunity for the entire family. Families need an information base that allows them to make reasonable relocation decisions. This book is intended to provide the essentials to achieve this goal.

Moving one's family is not easy, and it is never fun. However, I believe that if the unknowns are minimized, moves become manageable and serve to expand one's horizons. Personally, my family and I believe that the people we met and the places we lived have enriched our lives in many, many ways. I hope your journey helps you to realize the same. I wish you all the best in your new home and in your new community.

*Beverly D. Roman*

# ACKNOWLEDGEMENTS

BR Anchor Publishing would like to thank the following individuals for their valuable contributions to this edition of *Relocation 101*.

Linda Brown was the Headquarters Air Force Relocation Policy Consultant until 2003 when she transferred to Headquarters United States Central Command as the Chief, Quality of Life, Education and Family Support for the Joint Combatant Command. She has been a military spouse for 35 years, traveling to over 15 locations worldwide. Linda states "Relocation is still a challenge, but the services available to families make the logistics manageable and the emotions tolerable."

Camp Lejeune Relocation Assistance Program Specialists also assisted with the military information in this book. With over 20 years of combined on-the-job and personal experience, these relocation specialists can readily identify with what military spouses and family members are enduring and better prepare them for their moves.

Joy Loverde, author of *The Complete Eldercare Planner*, Second Edition (Times Books) offers advice on the subject of caring for elderly family members on pages 59-60. Joy's book includes checklists, communication tips on talking about sensitive subjects, The Documents Locator™, record-keeping forms, important questions to ask the doctor and more. Joy works with individuals who want to lessen the financial and emotional stresses of caring for elderly loved ones and with companies that want to attract and retain productive employees. For more information, visit Joy's website at www.elderindustry.com

# Relocation 101
**Making the Most of Your Move**

# CONTENTS

**RELOCATION OVERVIEW**     11 - 15
   PRESENTING THE MOVE
   CULTURAL CHANGE
   NEW HOME INFORMATION
   MILITARY MOVES
   SPECIAL MOVING SCENARIOS (Single parents, retirement and grandparents raising grandchildren)

**ORGANIZATION**     17 - 19
   GARAGE SALES
   FURNITURE MEASUREMENTS/ROOM PLANS
   RESERVATIONS

**FACT FINDING TRIP**     21
   FAMILIARIZE YOURSELF

**REAL ESTATE AGENTS**     23 - 24
   WHAT YOUR AGENT CAN DO FOR YOU
   AGENT SELECTION TECHNIQUES

**HOME SALES**     25 - 29
   REALISTIC PRICING
   HOME FACT SHEET
   POINTS THAT MAKE A DIFFERENCE
   VACANT HOMES
   RENTING INSTEAD OF SELLING

**RELOCATION INSURANCE**     31 - 32
   INSURANCE COVERAGE
   ANTIQUES AND COLLECTIBLES
   MOVING SPECIAL WINES

## Home Purchases     33 - 35
- Prequalifying and Preapproval
- Buyer Brokers
- Home Inspections/Warranties
- Building a Home
- Condominium Purchases

## Renting     37 - 39
- Lease Provisions
- Renter's Rights and Responsibilities

## Bank/Finance     41 - 42
- Comparing Banks
- Deductible Moving Expenses

## Career Opportunities     43 - 44
- Employee Benefits

## Spouse Relocation     45 - 49
- Develop a Plan
- Avenues of Assistance
- Employment Alternatives
- Male Career Interrupted Spouses
- Military
- Summing It Up

## Youth Corner     51 - 54
- Emotional Factors
- Evaluating New Schools
- Children and School Safety
- Choosing Child Care
- Alternative to Moving Students

## New Medical Care     55 - 56
- Individuals with Disabilities
- Medical Insurance

## Elder Care Options     57 - 58
- Making the Decision

| | |
|---|---|
| **ELDER CARE** by Joy Loverde | 59 - 60 |
| BEFORE YOU MOVE | |
| CAREGIVING FROM FAR AWAY | |
| **MOVING COMPANIES** | 61 - 62 |
| SELECTION CHECKLIST | |
| INSURANCE | |
| WORKING WITH THE MOVERS | |
| **SELF-HELP MOVING** | 63 - 64 |
| REQUIRED SUPPLIES | |
| PACKING AND LOADING | |
| **THE LAST DETAILS** | 65 - 68 |
| ITEMS TO TAKE WITH YOU | |
| DEPARTURE DAY ESSENTIALS | |
| DEPARTURE DAY | |
| **MOVING ON...** | 69 - 70 |
| TRAVEL PRECAUTIONS | |
| **MOVING IN** | 71 - 74 |
| YOUR NEW COMMUNITY | |
| SETTLING INTO A NEW HOME | |
| MAINTAINING CONTINUITY | |
| **REFERENCE SECTION** | 77 - 111 |
| This section will help you quickly organize relocation tasks. The checklists cover everything from medical topics and home sale transactions to pets and *more*. | |
| **INTERNET DIRECTORY** | 113 - 121 |
| **ABOUT THE AUTHOR** | 123 |
| **BOOKS IN PRINT** | 124 |
| **CONTACT INFORMATION/ORDERS** | 125 |

# RELOCATION OVERVIEW

Now that you have made the decision to relocate, there are issues to address early in your pre-move planning. If you have children, consider that they adapt to changes in different ways according to their ages, personalities, grade levels and involvements. Think about how your family has managed other moves, major lifestyle changes and/or separations when you plan your move. Initiate discussions, be attentive and take extra care with anyone with special concerns.

If you are in a dual career relationship, you need to consider the possibility of losing one salary and benefits as a result of the move. This is the time to evaluate your options and approach respective employers for assistance. *See* "Spouse Relocation" for avenues of assistance.

Throughout my family's 18 moves, we experienced many challenges including short- and long-term separations due to the nature of the assignment, school schedules and sometimes delayed home closings. While there are certainly inevitable situations associated with relocation, I believe that with enough preparation and information, people can avoid many relocation challenges and smooth their transitions.

## PRESENTING THE MOVE

As soon as you have made the decision to relocate, discuss the move with your children and any family members who will be directly affected by the transition. Before your discussion, try to anticipate possible concerns and questions.

Children will know if you and your spouse are not in agreement about the relocation decision, so be sure to explain the move to them in a unified and positive way, as appropriate for each child's age. Being informed is extremely important to children, so even if they are quite small, carefully review your moving plans and tell your children how you are going to work together to make the move become a positive experience and how you believe it can benefit the entire family.

## CULTURAL CHANGE

Relocation affects some people more profoundly than others. People have told me that they experienced feelings of sadness, anger and/or frustration as a result of moving from one community to another—*within the same city!* What these people experienced was cultural change, or what is commonly referred to as "culture shock." Although culture shock is generally associated with international moves, an often overlooked reality is that moving within and around a country, such as from a large metropolis to a rural community or from one ethnic area to another, can trigger this reaction as well.

To minimize the effects of cultural change, prepare your family by learning everything that you can about the new city. You especially want to evaluate the cost of living (i.e., travel, recreation, telephone, insurance, food, clothing and real estate). If the costs are substantially higher than what you are presently spending, discuss the differentials with your relocation manager. Other points to check are safety issues, weather/climate, sports teams, available activities and pastimes, customs, dialects and anything that you believe may affect your family.

## NEW HOME INFORMATION

The Internet is one of the most extensive resources for learning about a community. Our INTERNET DIRECTORY will get you started, plus you can investigate specific topics such as your new city or company. If you do not have a computer, you can use the facilities at public or university libraries. If you are an Internet novice, begin by logging onto the Internet and then type in a keyword for the subject that you want to find or use two words separated by "and" or the plus sign. When searching websites, I recommend that you accept and use information from recognizable and credible sources.

Look for relocation packages in your new community. Some Chambers of Commerce or Visitor Centers offer them, and most real estate agencies will provide packets of city-related information. Making the effort to become familiar with a location before you move will help your family slip into the new community much more easily.

# MILITARY MOVES

When enlisted personnel and officers are given orders to move to a new duty station, the move must generally be completed within a very short time frame. With the help of *Relocation 101*, you can make such knowledgeable decisions as whether to live on or off base, send your children to public or Department of Defense schools, hire a moving company and much more in a cost-effective and timely manner.

In addition to this book, there are many resources available to assist you with your move. Be sure to immediately contact the relocation manager at your base and access the military resources available on the Internet, especially SITES listed in our INTERNET DIRECTORY. SITES will help you learn everything you need to know about your new base, and then some. If you do not have a computer, you can access the Internet at a number of base facilities such as the library or the relocation office. Also, request special military discounts from every service provider that you use, such as moving companies and mortgage lenders.

If you are moving to a civilian community after living on base, keep in mind that the atmosphere and attitudes of these areas may be quite different from those with which you are familiar.

# SPECIAL MOVING SCENARIOS

### SINGLE PARENTS

For singles and single parent families, moving requires even more planning. As a single, you need to locate support systems and create friendships outside the traditional family unit; therefore, it is critical that you understand as much as possible about the new community. Be sure that the social life, activities, culture and pastimes to which you are accustomed will be available in the new community. If you are moving at the request of your employer, ask for help in locating services and other needs.

For singles with children, schools and/or day care facilities need special consideration as well. For instance, ask if there are provisions for children whose parents are delayed after normal child center hours.

Depending on your work commitments, you might consider hiring a nanny or someone to assist you with transportation to and from school and for unforeseen events or emergencies. Be sure to check out "Parents Without Partners, Incorporated" in the Internet Directory.

In addition, consider

- the support systems the children will have in another location,
- the custodial rights and the legal ramifications of moving children across state boundaries,
- how a move will affect the interaction between extended family members and your children.

### Retirement

Moving is challenging at any age, but if you move as you approach retirement, it takes special consideration. If the transition is not successful, relocating again is not only unsettling, disappointing and difficult—it is also very expensive. Your goal is to carefully evaluate the prospective area and everything about it that could impact you and your standard of living. You should also check on whether there is a Continuing Care Retirement Community (CCRC) in the area.

Visit communities you are considering during different seasons of the year to be sure you will be able to adjust to changes in climate and the community. For instance, some retirement communities are also resort communities and can be inundated with visitors during the "peak season," making it difficult to access restaurants, theaters and other activities.

Sometimes when people retire, they consider returning to the home town they left perhaps 20 or 25 years ago. These individuals have to keep in mind that although they believe they will be returning to a familiar lifestyle and environment, their former home may no longer feel that way. In the years of their absence, everyone will have changed in many ways. People moving back to a home community have to expect to rebuild friendships, as well as understand that former friends may feel ill at ease talking to people who have traveled all over the country and perhaps around the world.

After establishing residence in a new community, especially if you have moved to a new state, have your existing estate planning documents reviewed and updated by an attorney. This includes Living Wills or Advance Health Care Declarations, Durable Powers of Attorney and your Will and/or Trust.

You will also need to provide a change-of-address form to the Social Security office and previous employer so your pensions and other paperwork can be forwarded to you.

*See also* "RETIREMENT CHECKLIST" in the REFERENCE SECTION and retirement websites in the INTERNET DIRECTORY.

**GRANDPARENTS RAISING GRANDCHILDREN**

Approximately three million children are now living in homes maintained by their grandparents. This situation impacts employee relocation because 42 percent of grandparents are working and of the ages that they could be asked to move.

Although employees may have the responsibility of grandchildren, they may not have the legal rights to move them across state borders. Other concerns are lack of eligibility for medical or dental care under the grandparents' health plan and school enrollment. Securing legal guardianship allows grandchildren to be eligible for their own medical benefits and also gives grandparents the right to enroll them in school.

Support Groups in various communities are an excellent resource for grandparents offering emotional, psychological and moral support. These groups can be found through the AARP Grandparent Information Center. Write: Grandparent Information Center, 601 E Street, NW, Washington, DC 20049 for more details, or check "GRANDPARENT SUPPORT GROUP" in the INTERNET DIRECTORY.

# ORGANIZATION

Before you engage a real estate agent or place your home on the market, prepare your home so that it will show to its best potential. Organize, clean, repair, paint or replace whatever is necessary to reach this goal. Critically view your home, inside and outside, as though you are seeing it through a buyer's eyes.

Next, organize and straighten closets, storage areas, the attic and basement so they appear larger and more useful. This is a perfect time to sort through your household goods and select items that you believe your family will never use again. Encourage your children to do the same with their own belongings. Articles that have outlived your family's usefulness can be sold in a garage sale or donated to a charitable organization. If you donate articles, ask for a receipt for income tax purposes. When you arrive at your next home you will be glad you tackled this chore! After emptying the 90th box, there is nothing worse than coming across miscellaneous items you don't need *plus* having to find a place to put all of them.

My motto for any move is to make lists! Write down everything that comes to mind in the way of errands, people to call or chores to be accomplished. You can assign tasks to everyone in the family, with respect to their age and ability. In the REFERENCE SECTION of this book, you will find numerous checklists with suggestions to help you achieve an organized and smooth move.

*See also* "HOME SALES."

## GARAGE SALES

If your schedule permits, a garage sale is a great way to dispose of unwanted items, make some money and decrease your unpacking chores. Choose a convenient weekend when you will have help from family or friends. Ask neighbors to join you. Multiple family sales attract more customers, cost less (you share the advertising expense) and are more fun. To quickly price items, mark your wares with different colored self-adhesive dots.

Prepare a chart that lists the prices the colored dots represent and post it in a convenient place for your customers to view. Know that the amount you can garner for a garage sale item may differ considerably from the retail price. If you are not sure about what to ask for your wares, attend neighborhood sales to get ideas of "garage sale pricing" before you begin.

## FURNITURE MEASUREMENTS/ROOM PLANS

This may sound like a time consuming and/or useless exercise, but if you have ever been the only person home on moving day (as I have), you will appreciate not having to put on your track shoes each time the movers ask you: "Where does this dresser/bed/sofa belong?"

To measure furniture, you need a yardstick, tape measure, pencil, paper and one assistant. Allow approximately one hour for the project. Write down the room and describe the furniture contents by height, width and depth. If you have time, you can draw and cut models of your furniture from sturdy paper or 3" x 5" cards using a scale of 1/4 inch equals 1 foot.

If you have unusually large items such as a pool table or piano, you can make a pattern by drawing the dimensions on a large cloth or an old bed sheet. These patterns can be taken with you on househunting trips and placed in rooms to obtain a realistic concept of the space they will consume.

After you have purchased a home, you can create a floor plan for each room. Draw the room to size (drafting paper works well) and arrange the cut outs (or draw in the pieces) on each room plan. Move the pieces around until you are satisfied that you have maximized the space. Put the floor plans aside until moving day, then place them in their respective rooms to orient the movers.

When we moved into our home after a tour in Europe, we used the above technique and our movers considered it to be the smoothest international move they ever made. Complete this procedure and you will save yourself an untold amount of time, hassles and wear and tear on your shoes.

# RESERVATIONS

Part of your early organization should include planning your family's relocation travel. Some arrangements must be made in advance, especially if you are moving during the peak season (mid May through September) or near a holiday. Pre-move planning will ensure a safe and (relatively) relaxing trip.

- Make hotel/motel reservations two to four weeks in advance.

- For airplane reservations, call at least four to six weeks in advance for the best prices. If anyone requires a special meal, request it when booking your reservation.

- Train travel reservations can be made 24 hours a day for the next day, or for months ahead. Call Amtrack 1.800.USA.RAIL.

- Depending on your proposed travel schedule, you may consider making hotel/motel arrangements for the night you move out of your home. Most people are exhausted after packing and cleaning; a good night's sleep will let you travel to the new home refreshed.

- Pet transportation needs to be booked early to arrange convenient and cooler flight times. Check with the airlines, the moving company or your veterinarian for travel guidelines regarding proper kennel size, food and water restrictions and the required licenses, certificates and vaccinations.

*Note:* Don't forget to schedule a health examination and order a new identification tag for your pet before you move.

# FACT FINDING TRIP

Most companies allow at least one pre-move excursion to the city to which their employees are moving. This trip should be used to locate not only a new home, but also necessary services and stores. Collect business cards and pamphlets of information everywhere you go.

Homes you consider should be within the school districts that your family requires. As you peruse houses, check out room sizes, particularly the family room, bedrooms and kitchens. Carry with you a camera, tape measure, note pad, pencil and a calculator. Take pictures of prospective homes, rooms, schools, the city and places of interest to show your children. Knowing measurements of your furniture, especially large pieces, will help you evaluate homes.

## FAMILIARIZE YOURSELF

The following will help you become familiar with the new community and prepare for emergencies.

- Locate hospitals, pharmacies and physicians.
- Plan trips to schools and speak with teachers and counselors. If possible, take along descriptions of your children's books, readers and special programs.
- Discover the location of services/businesses and all the places of interest that are relevant to your family.
- Inquire about the city or state rules for importing pets, plants and food.
- Check out the methods of public transportation and places to obtain a new driver's license.
- Look into local Internet Service Providers (ISP's) so you can easily keep in touch with family and friends after the move.

*Note:* Review "HOME PURCHASES" in this book before your trip.

# REAL ESTATE NOTES

# REAL ESTATE AGENTS

Professional multi-list real estate firms and experienced real estate agents should help you to realize the best price for your home. Real estate firms offer services that individuals do not have access to on their own, such as placing homes in the Multiple Listing Service (MLS). Homes listed in MLS will be made known to an extensive list of real estate firms and clients.

## WHAT YOUR AGENT CAN DO FOR YOU

- Apprise you of the latest real estate legislation and taxes.
- Establish a realistic price for your home.
- Promote, advertise and show your home.
- Arrange for broker opens.
- Know how and where to seek prospective buyers.
- Schedule necessary inspections and appraisals.
- Provide a sound marketing plan.
- Create and mail professional promotional materials.
- Coordinate the closing of the sale.

## AGENT SELECTION TECHNIQUES

Ask a business colleague or a friend to recommend a real estate agent, preferably someone who has used the person's services in the past. Look for a representative who is: pursuing sales, returning telephone calls, aggressively working in his or her clients' best interests and whose only job is real estate. Select an agent who is familiar with home sales in your price range and in your desired neighborhoods. During your initial interview, ask about the agent's credentials, licensing and areas of expertise and request the agency's relocation information package. Following is a checklist of questions to help you select an agent.

- Do you have three satisfied clients of comparable properties to give us? Qualify all references.
- What percentage of the asking price, on average, have you received for the homes you've sold during the last year?
- What is the average number of days your listed homes were on the market?
- What types of homes do you typically sell?
- What advertising methods do you use? (Examples are targeted mailings, brochures, telephone calls and open houses.)
- How successful were your previous marketing efforts?

After you have selected an agent, ask for a marketing plan for your property outlining what will be involved and the frequency of marketing efforts. A most important step for you as the homeseller is to prepare detailed information to maximize your agent's home selling efforts. *See* "HOME FACT SHEET" for recommended specifics to provide.

There are hundreds of thousands of real estate agents in the United States alone, all with varying amounts of experience and expertise. You want to work with an agent with whom you feel comfortable and who will prepare a sound marketing plan for your home. If you take your time when selecting an agent and ask the suggested questions, you will minimize the hassles and maximize your profits.

*See also* "BUYER BROKERS" for alternative agents.

# HOME SALES

Profitable home sales begin with planning and preparation. Have your home priced right for the market and show it to its best advantage. Well-maintained homes are appealing to home buyers and discerning sellers recognize what motivates buyers.

## REALISTIC PRICING

Don't "test the market." Houses that are priced too high at the outset discourage buyers, and a seller can end up losing 10 to 20 percent on the sale. A qualified real estate agent or an appraisal firm can aid you in establishing a selling price while keeping in mind the amount of equity you need for your next purchase. If you have a limited amount of time to sell your home, work closely with your real estate agent to obtain an optimum price while expediting the sale.

Whoever evaluates your home should be aware of upgrades, renovations, items of particular value and negotiable points. Other factors that influence pricing include the current real estate market and the state of the economy. For instance, homes need to be priced competitively if the mortgage interest rates are low and the market is flooded with new homes.

If there is a lot of new construction in your community, consider that resales usually occur at prices below these homes. Also, buyers choose resale over new construction only if it is priced right.

Learn recent prices received for similar neighborhood homes. Real estate agents should be aware of these, but if not, inquire about home sales in your area at your county government office.

To avoid unnecessary hassles, be sure you specify that you only want to show your home to buyers who are qualified to purchase your property. See "PREQUALIFYING AND PREAPPROVAL."

# HOME FACT SHEET

The following details will help the real estate agent do a better job for you. Add whatever else is relevant to your situation.

- attributes that distinguish your home from others in the neighborhood
- average utility costs
- maintenance records and warranties
- description of features of the home, property and neighborhood
- annual property taxes
- history of services, including purchased warranties
- a list of all repairs and renovations to your home, especially those that have long-term benefits to a home buyer (such as upgrading and modernizing a kitchen)
- a list of schools, public transportation and churches
- a list of neighborhood activities, parks and recreation

Buyers are generally looking for energy-efficient homes in quiet neighborhoods with adequately sized lots. They want access to good schools as well as a low crime rate so be sure potential buyers know that your house fulfills these requirements.

# POINTS THAT MAKE A DIFFERENCE

### CURB APPEAL

Many people drive by a house before they make an appointment to see it; therefore, the first impression is critical. A well-maintained exterior entices a buyer to venture inside. Trees, shrubs and lawns should be well-manicured and if you need to improve these areas, know that experts consider landscaping to be a 200 percent return on investment.

Pay attention to other details as well because they can make a difference to selective buyers, especially during a difficult home market. Polish your front door handle, knocker and other brass accessories (replace if necessary), and be sure windows, shutters and sills are clean. If you're unable to fix something, do not intentionally disguise it from the prospective buyer because this could lead to a legal case for false advertising.

## STEPPING INSIDE

The second critical impression! Think about what first attracted you to your home. Emphasize these features and arrange furniture and decorations to enhance that effect.

Be sure that there are no noticeable smoking or pet odors and repair and replace any damaged fixtures. Many small problems can be repaired inexpensively, and the time and money spent will be amply returned.

Househunters will open closets, ovens, utility areas, cabinets, drawers and anything that has a door or handle. All the nooks and crannies in your home need to be tidy. If you have a closet or an area that is especially small, minimize the contents or furniture so that the areas will appear larger.

When your home is being shown, be available to answer questions but allow your agent and buyer privacy to view your home. A prudent exercise is to place valuables such as jewelry out of sight or in a safety deposit box during these visits.

*See also* "HOME SALE CHECKLISTS" in the REFERENCE SECTION.

## NEGOTIATING THE TRANSACTION

You can negotiate any home sale, home or condominium purchase or rental transaction. Many aspects can enter into the equation, so carefully evaluate each situation. A few points to consider are the time of year, whether or not there is an abundance of homes or rental units and whether the listings are brand new or more than six months old.

As a seller you can offer appliances as negotiable items, but they need to be up-to-date and in good working condition. Stoves, dishwashers and trash compactors are usually included in a home sale. Examples of negotiating tools are

- removable items such as microwaves, refrigerators, clothes washers and dryers;

- the cost of small repairs and/or paint;
- inspections and warranties;
- an allowance for carpeting, drapery or items that generally sell with the home that are in need of replacement.

## VACANT HOMES

If you are unable to sell your home before you move, you would be wise to take a few precautions because vandalism of empty homes is not uncommon. Most important is that your home appears occupied, so arrange for someone to periodically check on your home. However, I suggest that you make all arrangements in person or by mail instead of leaving messages outside because it signals that no one is home. Also let your insurance agent know your home will be vacant because your premium may need to be adjusted.

### Aspects to consider

- a well-maintained exterior and interior
- routine management of lawns, shrubs and/or snow removal
- inside and outside illumination
- periodic adjustment of drapery or blinds
- mail and deliveries removed from outside of the house
- automatic devices such as attic fans should be turned to the off position because they can be a fire hazard
- dampness or extreme temperatures can damage woodwork or appliances, so select a preferred house temperature

*Note:* As compensation for home supervision, I suggest you give your friends something that you know they would enjoy, such as a gift certificate to a restaurant of their choice.

## RENTING INSTEAD OF SELLING

If you do not need the cash from your present home at this time and prefer to rent it, use these suggested arrangements.

- Contract a real estate agent to screen potential tenants.

- Make arrangements with local service people, such as a plumber, electrician and heating contractor for routine and emergency repairs.
- Hire a property manager if you will reside too far away to make routine visits.
- Make finding a good tenant a high priority.

If you plan to sell the rental home in the future, be aware that there are certain tax advantages and/or exclusions with regard to the sale of this residence. Circumstances such as the length of time of home ownership, marital status, employment situation, principal residence category and other property ownership all can make a difference in your tax preparation. As tax laws change annually, you should contact your accountant to discuss the details of this important benefit.

# NOTES

# RELOCATION INSURANCE

Before you select a moving company and insurance coverage, you need to place a dollar amount on your household belongings. It is up to you to evaluate your goods so that you will be fully insured. I highly recommend that you begin insurance evaluation by completing a full inventory of everything you own. In addition, create records with photographs or a narrated descriptive home video. The inventory and photographs along with qualified appraisals will provide proof of ownership and condition in case of damage or loss. Your moving company will inventory your goods as well, but the contents may not be as specific. For instance, a box could be marked "dining room china" without noting the china manufacturer or the number of place settings.

As a side note, thousands of dollars worth of our household goods were irreparably damaged during one of our moves. When settling the insurance claim, the narrative home video we prepared prior to our move substantiated our losses.

## INSURANCE COVERAGE

Your employer will most likely provide a certain amount of insurance coverage. If you believe that you need to supplement this coverage, you can do so through the moving company or from your own insurance agent. Specifically request Replacement Cost insurance which will cover household goods for their current replacement value.

Ask your insurance agent to review your circumstances and outline the best homeowner policy for your situation. Ask about an insurance floater, a rider policy for high value items or an umbrella policy. The latter may give you better protection at a lower rate. Also find out if your current insurance will be applicable in the new location. If not, compare several other companies' policies and rates and obtain coverage before you move.

Finally, give your new address and relocation dates to your insurance agent and if you move before your home is sold, ask about the premiums for vacant homes.

*See also* "HOME SALES."

## ANTIQUES AND COLLECTIBLES

For high-priced collectibles such as antiques, art, jewelry, furs, silver and china, you should have authentic documentation. The original receipt (for recent purchases) or a current appraisal from an acceptable source, such as an antique dealer, will be adequate. Look under "Appraiser" in the Yellow Pages to find someone to value your antiques or call the American Society of Appraisers at 1.800.272.8258 for a recommendation. Carry valuations with you when you move.

Let your moving company representative know about any fragile or antique furniture. You can request to have these pieces crated for moving, but realize that crating adds weight which increases the cost of your move. Thick padding can serve to protect most furniture as well.

## MOVING SPECIAL WINES

Whether you have a wine collection or only a few special bottles, relay this information to your mover and ask about whether there are restrictions for transporting wines into your destination state.

The best temperature for storing and transporting wines is 55 degrees; therefore, if you are moving mid-summer, ask what the mover's provisions are for these goods. Photograph and inventory all the wines you plan to transport, detailing the amounts, types and values. If you do not know their current value, you can have them appraised by a knowledgeable wine merchant. Give a copy of the complete inventory to your mover.

# HOME PURCHASES

Give your agent your requirements for a home, along with a conservative price range. Detail your family's needs: school requirements, interests and activities, transportation, a home office and work locations. Outline a realistic mortgage budget and factor in the possibility of a future move. For important purchase details, and to compare prospective homes, see "HOME PURCHASE CHECKLISTS."

Whether or not you have children, look for homes that have an excellent school district for future resale value. Also neighborhoods with homes that are similar in size and price will more readily hold their value and be attractive for resale.

## PREQUALIFYING AND PREAPPROVAL

To expedite a home purchase, become preapproved before you shop. If you shop for a mortgage first, you will have a more realistic idea of the terms and conditions that are available, as well as the amount of money for which you qualify.

Becoming prequalified is a fairly informal process and it will improve your bargaining power with sellers. Potential lenders will check your credit and employment history and verify down payment funds. The lender will then write a letter (often a form letter) stating that based on the information presented to them, the buyer is prequalified. Following this step, you can become preapproved, which will assure you financing for a certain dollar amount on an appropriate property. Preapprovals are relatively inexpensive and can be procured prior to your househunting trip.

If you are in a hurry to buy, do not disclose your timing and never disclose your financial information. At the same time, if you can learn the seller's situation (whether they are anxious to move or if they need the funds for a down payment) you may have more negotiation leverage.

## BUYER BROKERS

In contrast to real estate agents who basically work for the seller, buyer broker agents work on the home buyer's behalf, helping them to make informed decisions. Buyer broker's services can include:

- explanation of property regulations and financing alternatives,
- access to all homes on the market, including those "For Sale by Owner,"
- research of comparable properties,
- access to full disclosure of the property history,
- disclosure of defects in the home(s) and recommending inspections,
- negotiations with the seller on your behalf while keeping your financial information confidential.

A buyer broker's community expertise and property insight can be very helpful to the home buyer. See EBASearch.com in the INTERNET DIRECTORY for a buyer broker in your area.

## HOME INSPECTIONS/WARRANTIES

More than 40 percent of previously owned homes have at least one serious defect so a home inspection is a prudent exercise for any home buyer. Call several inspection firms for prices and lists of their services and select an inspector based on experience, not on price alone. Inspections are an important part of home purchases so plan to accompany the inspector and take notes.

In addition, know that homes built prior to 1978, and especially before 1960, could contain lead-based paint. For these homes, I definitely recommend hiring a professional building inspector to check the home's structure and appliances, plus check for lead or radon problems.

A home warranty can be an important sales tool, especially in a slow resale market. Warranties cover the major appliances sold with the home, heating and air conditioning systems and the water heater, usually for one year. This is especially important for older homes.

Warranties, like inspections, vary. Some are more inclusive than others and some have deductibles so ask several companies for detailed information about their plans, services, prices and special offers.

*See also* "HOME INSPECTIONS" in the REFERENCE SECTION.

## BUILDING A HOME

If you do not find a home on the market that meets your needs, you may consider building. Building provides an opportunity to plan a home for your family's present and future needs and lifestyle. Also, building allows you to have the most up-to-date features and styling which makes homes easier to sell and thus worth consideration if you anticipate another move.

If you choose to build a home, you will have to locate interim living accommodations because it takes 10 months or more to complete a home. Plus you have to consider that inclement weather, unavailable subcontractors or out-of-stock materials can lengthen the building schedule.

## CONDOMINIUM PURCHASES

Condominiums and townhouses offer privacy similar to that of a home, with less maintenance and responsibility. However, these units do not always come with conveniences such as a garage or covered parking. Evaluate this purchase option as you would a home and have it inspected as well. Find out the appraised value so you do not pay more than a unit is worth. Know the number of empty units in the complex, how they are selling and the amount of appreciation. Note the way the grounds are kept, the interior design and the floor plan. If you believe you may soon move again, it is important that the complex you choose has a history of profitable and swift sales.

*See also* "NEW CONSTRUCTION/CONDOS" in the REFERENCE SECTION.

# NOTES

# RENTING

Some people want the flexibility that renting affords, others are encouraged to do so by their employers and still others simply do not want the responsibility of owning a property. If you are shopping for a rental accommodation, visit homes or complexes during different times of the day to get a true picture of the atmosphere, noise level, lifestyle and safety. If you have a home-based business and are considering an apartment as your next home, look into facilities that offer business centers in their complexes. Know that when you rent you will have to purchase separate insurance because the landlord's policy will not cover your personal property, clothes, furniture or valuables. Consider the length of time you will be living in the rental, as well as the following points.

## CONSIDERATIONS

- room sizes and closet space
- protected parking areas
- bicycle storage
- patios (use and storage and whether grills are allowed)
- the number of cars a tenant may park on the premises
- whether the office complex accepts deliveries
- the frequency of refurbishing and painting by the landlord
- timely replacement of air conditioning and heating filters
- timely lawn care and snow removal
- well-maintained building and grounds
- rental activity (units occupied versus empty units)
- available transportation

- realistic pricing, monthly fees (utility, maintenance and club) plus frequency and amount of rental increases
- distance to work and your favorite pastimes
- age and condition of appliances, heating/AC systems and plumbing
- availability of the landlord for maintenance service (even after office hours)
- adequate insulation and storm windows

## LEASE PROVISIONS

Leases will vary, but they all need to include the following:

- names of the tenant and landlord;
- correct rental property address, including your house or unit number;
- the dollar amount of rent, the due date, where and to whom to make the payments;
- the length of time the lease is valid and the timing to renew the lease;
- charges for late rental payments;
- who is responsible for the utility payments, i.e., water, sewage, electricity and gas;
- policies for garbage removal and recycling;
- pool and clubhouse access hours and fees;
- rules and deposits for pets;
- security deposit (amount and conditions for its return);
- changes (drapery/paint) that may be made in the house or apartment and the party responsible for costs;
- a "Notice to Terminate" section that may allow you to end the lease early without financial penalties with proper notification and qualifications.

# RENTER'S RIGHTS AND RESPONSIBILITIES

Thoroughly check the entire home or apartment before signing a lease. If you find any defects and/or damages, document them with dated pictures.

Landlords are required to make an appointment with you to enter your home or apartment while you are away. If it is necessary for a landlord to enter during your absence, a note should be left indicating that someone was in your dwelling and the purpose of the visit.

### Negotiating tips

If there are an abundance of rental units, or you sense that the landlord wants to fill the accommodation, think about asking for one or more of the following:

- one month's free rent
- new or refurbished appliances
- new paint and/or wallpaper
- free pool access
- new carpeting
- a shorter lease

Just as with home purchases, rental agreements can be negotiated. Consider your personal situation, as well as the landlord's, before signing on the dotted line.

As a final note, be sure to ask to have your security deposit returned to you when you move.

# NOTES

# BANK/FINANCE

Establish banking services in your new location before you move by sending a check via registered or certified mail to the appropriate bank source. Doing this will make it easier to have your checks accepted by local merchants and if you regularly use automated teller machines (ATMs), you may avoid the fees charged to access funds.

## COMPARING BANKS

When comparing banks, note whether their branches and ATMs are convenient to your home, office and shopping areas. Ask about the banks' services because they can vary from one institution to another and some offer some unique services such as home or apartment assistance for new customers. Be sure you are fully established with the new bank before terminating former accounts.

### SERVICES TO COMPARE

- account maintenance fees and applied interest
- an automatic deposit system
- hours of operation
- online services
- overdraft protection
- savings programs or special personal services
- a 24-hour toll-free number
- affiliations with international services such as HONOR, Cirrus and Plus
- withdrawal limits for ATMs
- free checking and safety deposit boxes

## DEDUCTIBLE MOVING EXPENSES

List yearly expenses and compare them with allowable moving deductible expenses in the Internal Revenue Service's "Moving Publication" #521. Current forms are available at post offices or through the IRS at www.irs.gov or 1.800.829.3676.

- Job search expenses
    - postage
    - telephone calls
    - interview travel costs
    - résumé printing costs
    - employment agency fees

- Moving expenditures
    - boxes and packing materials
    - meals, lodging, travel (gas, tolls)
    - babysitting and child care
    - transportation of an automobile
    - in-transit storage
    - kennel fees

- Out-of-pocket expenses for volunteer work

- Articles that are donated to charitable organizations

Some of the points that can make a difference in tax dollars are

- time of year;

- military, retiree and marital status;

- two income returns, self-employment and work related moves;

- housing costs and distances traveled to work.

If you sold a home and bought another, some expenses can be claimed on your income tax. However, it may be more lucrative to claim these same costs as moving expenses instead of home transaction expenses. Check with an accountant to evaluate your personal circumstances. Any employer reimbursements must be claimed as income.

*See also* "CAREER OPPORTUNITIES" and "HOME SALES."

# CAREER OPPORTUNITIES

Continuity of work efforts and attitudes will positively impact your goals in your new assignment. Be sure you review your responsibilities with your predecessor before assuming the new position. Also be aware of

- your new title and authority,
- how quickly you could move again,
- the skills you can gain from this position,
- how your acquired skills will be utilized in future corporate planning.

When working in a satellite office, it is important to stay involved with mainstream operations.

- Make your accomplishments known to key personnel.
- Watch for career opportunities.
- Prioritize your personal efforts.
- Arrange for your interaction in company projects and events.
- Stay tuned into corporate developments, changes in products and policies, present and future business strategies and the culture/climate within the company.
- Make any unique challenges known to your superiors which will assist them with future corporate planning.

## EMPLOYEE BENEFITS

Continuation of benefits should be discussed with your employer before you move. Some points to explore are

- medical coverage,
- professional organizations and/or other memberships,

- holidays and vacations,
- training opportunities.

Additionally, think about the possibility of not being able to sell your home before you move. Some companies purchase homes from transferred employees or defray the costs of a dual mortgage. In addition, more and more companies are covering costs relating to

- career assistance for your spouse,
- travel to find a new home,
- temporary housing,
- installation fees (cable, utility, Internet access),
- buyout of automobile leases.

Be sure that you have a complete understanding of the expenses your employer will assume, as well as those for which you will be responsible.

# SPOUSE RELOCATION

If you are a working spouse and your partner has accepted a job transfer, you need to evaluate your own career and develop a strategy based on your personal and professional needs.

## DEVELOP A PLAN

Think about maintaining your career in the new community. With a fax machine, e-mail account and express mail, many employees successfully telecommute to the corporate office. Approach your employer with suggestions to maintain your position from another city and be open to discuss your employer's proposals as well. If your employer is not enthusiastic about you working from afar, perhaps you can negotiate a trial period for the plan, agreeing on reasonable terms and conditions. If it is possible that you may return to live in this community, your employer may be amenable to you taking a leave of absence for the purpose of furthering your education or skills.

If you are unable to relocate your career, this presents an opportunity to reassess your personal and professional goals. To begin this process, ask yourself: do I want to

- pursue my current career at its present level?
- seek advancement in my current field?
- seek training in another field?
- pursue an advanced degree or further training?
- seek a different type of position using my developed skills?
- work part-time or obtain temporary employment?
- start my own business?

If you are changing course, begin by asking yourself the following questions:

- What skills and accomplishments do I have that are transferrable?

- How have my skills been demonstrated on and off the job?
- What do I most enjoy doing?
- In what areas have I been most successful?
- What methods worked best for me in my former position(s)?
- What are my greatest strengths? My talents?

Next, evaluate how you can use all of this information to create or further a new career. If you decide to seek another position, you need to compose a new résumé that conveys your skills, accomplishments and strengths. If you are rusty on résumé writing or interview skills, locate a career counseling service that offers these services.

## AVENUES OF ASSISTANCE

### Corporations

Increasing numbers of corporations are recognizing the challenges that two income families face. Therefore, your partner's company may offer spouse assistance. Corporations can make résumés available to other companies, assist with résumé rewrites, find a job within the company or provide career counseling. Employees need to outline their family situations and have provisions written into the relocation package.

### Newspapers

Subscribe to the Sunday edition of the new town's newspaper before you move. This will allow you to become familiar with the major industries in the new community and learn which companies are hiring.

### Real estate agencies

Many agencies now have a "Partner Career Assistance Program" which can arrange interviews to coincide with your first househunting trip. If this program is not available, ask the agency to refer you to an independent career counselor.

### Universities

Your alma mater's career placement office may offer career counseling services to its alumni. Contact the counselor at your former institution for information and set up an interview, either in person or by telephone (most institutions are also on the Internet).

### Employment counselors

To contact a counselor on your own, look under "Career," "Employment" or "Vocational" in the Yellow Pages. Counselors will find contacts within your field or assess your marketable skills for a possible career/job change. Most counselors have contacts with local businesses in their respective communities.
Ask prospective counselors if they

- give advice to allow their customers flexibility in job hunting,
- are equipped to offer a range of job related services, i.e., networking, preparing cover letters and résumés and helping clients develop interview skills,
- will provide telephone counseling when necessary,
- will arrange regular follow-ups until an appropriate placement is found,
- have a wide base of contacts in the community to whom you can be referred (ask to see examples of the research they perform for clients),
- are realistic in saying what they can accomplish (beware of guarantees).

### The internet

"Dual Career" in the Internet Directory lists valuable sites to search for positions, register résumés, compare salaries and answer questions.

### Temporary employment agencies

Some of these agencies teach basic office skills at no cost or for a nominal fee. In addition, temporary jobs sometimes turn into permanent positions which can offer benefits and security.

## EMPLOYMENT ALTERNATIVES

Take a sabbatical to enroll in some courses or volunteer your time and talent to a local or national organization. Both of these efforts can embellish your portfolio. Most city newspapers list volunteer opportunities on a weekly basis. Courses are also available on the Internet and can be used to obtain certification or a diploma. Internships are still another consideration if you want to work but do not want a full-time position. You can offer to work the number of hours of your choice at no cost to the company while you are gaining new experience and skills. A break in work can also provide a wonderful time to just be with the family, or start a family.

## MALE CAREER INTERRUPTED SPOUSES

More and more women are obtaining executive positions and accepting transfers. Plus companies are downsizing and the overall job scenarios are changing as more men find themselves looking for a job, working in an entirely new capacity and/or working from home. Therefore, the male accompanying spouse issue has the potential to become another significant dual career concern.

This role reversal is often difficult for men because they have traditionally been regarded as the breadwinners in most societies. Even though the thought of being free of work demands may sound enticing at first, men may experience feelings of depression and must realize that adaptation can take six months or more. Couples in this situation may need to redefine their roles for themselves, as well as for their children. Children need to have a clear understanding why their parents have chosen this lifestyle.

Men need to prepare for pressures that may confront them in their non-traditional roles. For example, some male peers will have difficulty accepting men who are willing to take on household and child care responsibilities. Other peers may simply feel uncomfortable in trying to relate to non-working men. Additionally, some of the activities and pastimes that female spouses enjoy may not interest stay-at-home men.

*Note:* The points in this chapter about job opportunities and job searches apply to men as well as women.

## MILITARY

Military spouses might have the opportunity to work on- or off-base. On-base opportunities often include civil service or military exchange (commissary) positions. Family Services, Community Services or Family Support offices also frequently have open positions. As soon as you know you are moving, visit your Transition Assistance Office and ask for a contact at the new base to learn about job opportunities, helpful websites and other resources for working spouses. You will especially want to visit "SITES" listed under "MILITARY" in this book's INTERNET DIRECTORY. Also input "Federal Consumer Information Center" into any search engine on the Internet. This site lists pamphlets on career training, employment, interview advice, health benefits, jobs of tomorrow and more.

## SUMMING IT UP

In addition to the suggestions in this chapter, tap every resource that is available, tell everyone you meet that you are job hunting and describe the position you are pursuing. Join clubs and/or volunteer your services to organizations and do as much networking as possible. You never know who may know of a position or contact person that may lead to a new job.

Even with assistance, job hunting is primarily a do-it-yourself project. The state of the economy, your career field, the community, your motivation level and timing will all influence how long it takes to become reestablished.

Career interrupted spouses need to implement a new routine so that each day has a purpose. Take advantage of everything the new community has to offer, get plenty of exercise and maintain a balance between home and outside activities.

# YOUTH CORNER

Creating a sound transition plan for the family is significant to achieving a successful move. Children will worry less about a move, and be more excited about the new city, if they are involved in the process. There are many things children can do to help you, while at the same time make moving more fun for them. A few suggested activities…

- Sort through their belongings for outgrown clothing and toys.
- Plan their new bedrooms.
- Learn about the new community with their parents.
- Help with the relocation travel plans and parents' lists.
- Take care of their pet's travel needs.
- Make lists of items that they will want to take on their trip.

### A FEW TIPS

Give your children a few activities to do on moving day, and give them a room to use that can easily be packed last. Also, a fun thing to do is to record yourself reading stories to your children. They can listen to these tapes on the relocation trip or any time when you are not with them.

## EMOTIONAL FACTORS

Don't underestimate the effects relocation can have on children, no matter what their "relocation history" has been. Listen carefully to each child's concerns and address them according to their age. Signs that children are struggling with an adjustment can include any combination of the following:

- sudden reading difficulties,
- changes in attention span or study habits,
- weight loss or gain,
- altered enthusiasm or energy levels,
- strained relationships with you or their siblings,

- disturbed sleep patterns.

### Helping children adjust

Encourage your children to stay in contact with former friends and family by exchanging pictures and letters. You can also establish an e-mail account for your family and purchase pre-paid telephone cards for children to use. If the distance is not too great, children can have exchange visits with friends during holidays or long weekends. Stay abreast of how your children are adjusting by discussing school and personal issues during routine family meetings.

## EVALUATING NEW SCHOOLS

Review your children's current educational materials, courses of study and educational plans before going school shopping. Most schools can be found on the Internet by typing "school and city" (use the name of your new city) in the search field. Here are significant points to consider when evaluating schools.

### School criteria

- accreditation rating
- faculty (experience and background)
- space availability
- course selection (remedial to advanced placement)
- language instruction
- standardized test scores, amount of university placements and national enrollments
- colleges and universities that graduates are attending
- academic programs of study
- graduation requirements
- school requirements
- up-to-date library
- classroom computers
- extracurricular activities, such as theater and creative groups, school publications and sports programs

To locate primary and secondary schools, higher education institutions and educational options look under "EDUCATION" in the INTERNET DIRECTORY. There is also a "SCHOOL FORM LETTER" in the REFERENCE SECTION.

## CHILDREN AND SCHOOL SAFETY

Understand the school's safety policy during school hours and for after-school activities. If you have young children, know if there is a before- and after-school program for their care.

- Explain to your children the rules and regulations for playground activities and how to deal with strangers.
- Be sure your children know the individuals from whom they can accept rides.
- Teach children their school bus number.
- Tell children to wait until the bus comes to a complete stop before entering or exiting.
- Have children enter and exit cars only at a close/safe area near the school.

Some schools have a means to care for new students such as a Welcome Club or a Buddy System. If neither are in place, you can be instrumental in establishing one.

## CHOOSING CHILD CARE

Visit at least three centers and interview instructors to evaluate the center's environment, cleanliness, values and capabilities.

**POINTS TO EVALUATE**

- state licensing and accreditation
- small teacher to pupil ratio
- teachers with training in early childhood education
- a bright and cheery environment that provides creative daily activities, a well-planned schedule and outdoor playtime
- children who seem comfortable and who are free to move about and investigate their surroundings

- children who are happily occupied and approach caregivers easily when they need help or attention
- compliance with fire and building safety codes
- nutritional lunches
- adequate emergency medical care procedures

Resource and Referral agencies, or R&Rs, are listed in telephone books. These agencies help parents locate and evaluate licensed child care centers, family day care homes and in-home caregivers. Child Care Aware assists in finding child care Resource and Referral agencies; call 1.800.424.2246.

*See also* "CHILD CARE" in the INTERNET DIRECTORY.

## ALTERNATIVE TO MOVING STUDENTS

Depending on your children's grades, ages and involvements, you may consider allowing them to remain in the same city with a trusted adult. Or, one parent may elect to stay behind with the children until they finish a grade level. Either option requires extended family efforts and preparation. Never assume your children know procedures for routine or emergency situations.

### CHILDREN SHOULD UNDERSTAND
- How to seek medical care and handle insurance
- Names and telephone numbers of relevant doctors
- Finances and expenditure limitations
- Methods to access funds for unexpected needs
- Dialing procedures for police, fire or ambulance
- How, when and where everyone will see each other
- The host family's expectations, including curfew guidelines
- School responsibilities
- Car and travel privileges

Everyone involved in this unique type of situation needs to agree on the above issues, plus any other relevant points.

# NEW MEDICAL CARE

Preventive medicine is still the best medicine. Before you move, prepare a complete medical file and schedule a physical, dental and eye examination for everyone in your family. Locate physicians and medical care facilities in the new area before you move or as soon as possible after you arrive. University affiliated hospitals are good sources to locate doctors, plus your personal physician may be able to recommend a colleague in or near your new town. Relocating to a new community places additional stress on families and, consequently, they are more vulnerable to accidents or illness. *Don't move unprepared!*

*See also* "MEDICAL CHECKLIST" and "NEW HEALTH SERVICES" in the REFERENCE SECTION. To locate a new doctor, check "MEDICAL" in the INTERNET DIRECTORY.

## INDIVIDUALS WITH DISABILITIES

If someone in your family requires special help, research the facilities and services that are available in the new location before you move. Organizations such as the Blind Association or the Multiple Sclerosis Society help families locate medical care and special services. These organizations also provide information about handicapped accessible places of worship, post offices, museums, banks and restaurants. Floor plans, handrails, walkways, ramps, doorway openings, seating arrangements and work accommodations all need to be taken into consideration.

Movers need to know the layout of your current and future homes, as well as any special moving requirements. Also discuss special needs equipment that has to be moved, the care it will require and the amount of dismantling and set up that will be involved. All equipment should be disassembled before the actual moving day to avoid last minute confusion and delayed schedules. If moving companies cannot take care of special needs equipment, most will arrange for an outside firm to do so.

# MEDICAL INSURANCE

Maintaining your health insurance is an important consideration when moving. If your family is insured through the transferred employee's company, you will want to guarantee continuation of coverage. Verify your new mailing address and telephone number with your company's benefits administrator, plus ask if any policy changes such as costs or benefits will take effect, particularly if you will be moving out-of-state.

If your family is insured through the spouse's former employer, you may be able to continue existing coverage for up to one year under state mandated continuation or for 18 months under Federal COBRA. However, limitations may apply and costs may vary if moving to another state. Once the continuation period is over, you will have to obtain new insurance for which you must be medically qualified. If you have had serious medical problems, most states require an insurance company to offer a COBRA conversion policy that takes over when COBRA ends.

If you have never had an employer sponsored insurance policy but instead have purchased an individual family plan, it is very important that you notify the insurance company of your new address and transfer your coverage to that location as soon as possible. If your current policy will not transfer out-of-state, you need to research the availability and costs of individual plans in the state to which you are moving.

The above information is merely an overview; please speak directly with your company's Human Resource department, benefits administrator and/or an insurance company customer service representative about your pending relocation to learn how the move will specifically affect your coverage.

# ELDER CARE OPTIONS

If you are caring for an elder relative *and* moving, long-term planning is crucial. First, realistically evaluate whether or not your relative can, or even wants to, move with you. If this is not an option, then you need to consider the amount and types of help your relative will require, as well as the support systems he or she will have in your absence.

## MAKING THE DECISION

If your relative currently lives with you and wants to move with your family, consider how this change could affect him/her, as well as your immediate and extended family members. Keep in mind that whether you are relocating a state away or across the country, people can experience varying levels of culture shock.

For elders who are currently living alone, families need to realistically evaluate whether or not they can continue to do so. For instance, can they independently manage daily chores, home care and finances? Options are provided in the next chapter for people who need home care assistance. To obtain a free brochure titled "How to Choose a Home Care Provider," send an 8.5x11 SASE to The National Association for Home Care and Hospice, Publications Department, 228 Seventh Street, SE, Washington, DC 20003 or call 202.547.7424.

Whether you choose a home care provider or an assisted living facility, I suggest that you request references from doctors, patients or family members who are familiar with the provider's quality of service. Be sure to visit several facilities before selecting one. And in both instances, ask how personnel are screened and how they follow up on and resolve problems that arise. Everyone's situation needs to be evaluated and quality care obtained no matter what living conditions you choose.

If you are moving a long distance from your relative, begin to lay plans for travel and time off from work. Consider saving family leave or personal days, making back-up child care plans and starting a travel fund. The 1993 Family Medical Leave Act may entitle you to up to 12 weeks of unpaid leave a year to care for an elderly relative. Many companies are now providing elder care assistance and resources so you should discuss your needs with your employer.

*See also* "Elder Care" in the Internet Directory regarding education, support and legal advice for elders and caregivers plus there is an "Eldercare Checklist" in the Reference Section.

# ELDER CARE
### By Joy Loverde

No doubt, moving is hectic but taking the time now to get organized and identify eldercare-related resources for long distance caregiving will be well worth the effort. If you haven't done so already, establish an e-mail account for each of your elderly loved ones. You'll want to be able to communicate with them in a flash no matter where you are.

## BEFORE YOU MOVE

**GET ORGANIZED** Create one file for each elderly family member. Use this file to store notes, medical/medications history, emergency telephone numbers and important documents. Make a copy of your elder's Social Security card, driver's license and proof of health insurance for the file. Complete the "ELDERCARE EMERGENCY CHART" in the REFERENCE SECTION. Provide copies of the chart to your elder relative, other family members and a trusted neighbor. Routinely update the information as necessary.

**CREATE PARTNERSHIPS** Surround your elders with people you can count on for big and little caregiving responsibilities—anything from making routine home visits to accompanying your relative to doctors' appointments. Be sure that you can reach helpers 24 hours a day, 7 days a week. Write down names, street and e-mail addresses, places of employment and home and cell phone numbers.

**ESTABLISH POWER OF ATTORNEY FOR FINANCES AND HEALTHCARE** Initiate a frank discussion with your relative about establishing Power of Attorney and Durable Power of Attorney for Healthcare. Documents must be completed and signed while the elderly person is of sound mind.

**CREATE ACCESS** Duplicate your elder's home, car and mailbox keys. Keep one set with you and distribute other sets to family members/caregivers. Write down access codes, passwords and combination lock codes for doors, gates, garages, computers, mailboxes, voice mail and telephone answering machines.

**BECOME AWARE OF IN-HOME CARE OPTIONS**  Most elderly people prefer to stay in their own homes for as long as possible. Contact the local Department on Aging to learn about the resources and services they have to offer.

## CAREGIVING FROM FAR AWAY

After you move, it is only natural that you will feel a certain amount of guilt and, at times helplessness, when you are far away. These feelings are normal, and a reminder of how important it is that you have several people back home you trust and can rely on to help carry out caregiving tasks and keep you up to date on what is taking place in your relative's life.

**MAKE RETURN TRIPS**  To ease your feelings of concern regarding elderly relatives, it will help if you periodically make home visits. In addition to spending time together, you'll be reassured that the eldercare plans you put in place are working to your satisfaction.

**KEEP IN TOUCH**  Stay connected as best you can, and share as much as possible about your life in your new city or country via frequent correspondence, telephone calls and e-mail.

**RESPOND TO AN ELDERCARE EMERGENCY**  In the event that your relative requires a different level of care after you relocate, connect with the caregivers and review the resources listed on the "Eldercare Emergency Chart." Talk to your elder's doctor and family members to find out if it is necessary for you to catch the next plane home.

If important decisions or changes must be made regarding care, include your elder in the decision-making process whenever possible.

Joy Loverde is a columnist, speaker and spokesperson for elder care issues. See page 4 for more about Joy and check our INTERNET DIRECTORY for websites regarding education, support and legal advice for elders and caregivers.

# MOVING COMPANIES

The moving company sales representative will be your contact person. He or she will tour your home with you, evaluate your shipment, request the appropriate number of packers, note the estimated weight of your goods and arrange for pick-up, delivery and storage dates. Inform the agent of items requiring special attention, such as antique furniture or fragile items. Ask for a written proposal detailing everything you discussed for your move, including special requests and extra services.

## SELECTION CHECKLIST

Compare prices, ask for personal references of satisfied customers and ask these people questions about the moving company's services. For instance: Did the movers use runners? Were they careful with the furniture? Did they provide you with realistic packing, pick up and delivery schedules? Were they courteous? You can also contact the Better Business Bureau for information.

**IMPORTANT CONSIDERATIONS**

- computerized tracking methods
- costs for packing, mileage and unloading
- on-time pick up and delivery records
- dry, clean and safe company storage facilities
- services and special discounts
- company performance records
- drivers' experience and reliability
- well-maintained trucks and equipment
- appropriate licenses
- applicable discounts

## INSURANCE

Understand the amount and type of insurance that is available, how insurance claims will be handled and the time limit you will have to file a claim. You should have a realistic idea of the value of your household goods after completing your inventory detailed in "Relocation Insurance." With this amount in mind, compare the moving company's insurance with your corporate plan for reimbursements to determine if you need additional coverage.

Read the moving company's Bill of Lading (a contract describing the goods to be shipped) before you sign it. Keep this form in a safe place until your household goods are delivered, charges are paid and any claims are settled.

### Rules and Regulations

- Know the rules for boxes packed by owner ("PBO"). If you pack a box and it arrives damaged, you can submit a claim for broken goods within; however, if the box is not damaged, broken items are your responsibility.

- Understand which materials cannot be moved, i.e., flammable or hazardous materials.

- Ask about the regulations for moving plants, foods and pets to your new location.

- After the inventory has been completed, review the notations about damaged goods to be sure you agree.

- Sign all moving company inventory forms.

## WORKING WITH THE MOVERS

Having made 18 moves, I suggest you begin by learning all the movers' names, find out who is in charge (usually the driver) and establish a good working relationship. Show the movers around your home, alerting them to special requirements, especially fragile items (on which you should have placed a large note marked "FRAGILE"). Remember, any good move is a cooperative effort between you and the movers.

### A few last notes

Most moving companies do not accept personal checks. Find out if you need a cashier check, traveler's check or money order.

Providing snacks, light meals or tips are not required. However, many people offer these as a courtesy. Ask your moving representative about the company's guidelines on these issues.

# SELF-HELP MOVING

Moving on your own requires more organization and packing on your part, and you will need to engage friends or relatives to assist you. Be sure the people you ask are dependable because time is money when renting equipment. A two hour delay could ultimately cost you an extra day's rental fee.

Next, compare three companies and ask for their free brochures about moving techniques. The brochures will give you comprehensive details about how to pack, load and secure household goods. When surveying companies, consider

- costs per day for truck, equipment and mileage;
- insurance and liability coverage;
- ease of pick up and delivery;
- type of rental equipment;
- extra services such as published literature, blankets, furniture ties and dollies for heavy appliances.

When renting a truck, you will need to know the number of rooms and storage spaces you will be packing. The rental company should be able to suggest the appropriate size truck you will need. If you are debating the size, rent one a little larger than you believe will be necessary because it is difficult to assess everything you really have in all those drawers and closets.

Understand the rental company's rules and warranties in case problems occur on the road, such as a flat tire or mechanical malfunctions. Obtain agreements in writing and know telephone numbers for service contacts and assistance.

## REQUIRED SUPPLIES

As soon as you know you are moving, begin to save whatever wrapping paper you can. Avoid using newspaper as the ink can stain your belongings. Scour your closets for old blankets or anything you can use to pad your furniture. You can also acquire boxes from convenience, book and grocery stores. Stock up on package sealing tape, marking pens and labels.

Self-help moving companies will have furniture ties, blankets and dollies for rent. The dollies will be especially helpful to move your appliances. You can also obtain used and new boxes, wardrobe containers, wrapping paper and other supplies from these companies.

## PACKING AND LOADING

Because moving on your own requires more preparation, start as soon as possible to pack anything that you do not routinely use, such as seasonal items. After you pack a box, mark it as completely as possible. Your short-hand designations may be forgotten by the time you arrive at your destination.

Begin your loading process by placing the heaviest furniture and appliances near the cab of the truck, packing them as tightly as possible. Tie a strong rope around the furniture from one side of the truck to the other approximately every quarter length of the truck. Refer also to literature from your self-help moving company for packing and loading advice, as well as our tips in "THE LAST DETAILS."

Finally, be sure you have adequate insurance coverage for your household goods. *See also* "RELOCATION INSURANCE."

# THE LAST DETAILS

This chapter suggests chores to be completed one or two weeks before the packers arrive on your doorstep. The more organized you are on moving days, the fewer hassles you will encounter.

- Put important documents such as airline tickets or personal records in a safe place so they are not inadvertently packed by the movers. I have been known to place necessities and records in the trunk of my car to avoid having them packed.
- Collect "ITEMS TO TAKE WITH YOU" listed on the next page.
- Place large signs on appropriate household goods. If there are any items that you will need immediately at the new home, mark them as "LAST ON." These could include the furniture, lamps and television/VCR for the family room. Additional labeling suggestions are "STORAGE," "DO NOT PACK," "FRAGILE" and "FOR IMMEDIATE USE."
- If you pack any of your belongings yourself, label the boxes with as many specific contents as possible. Try not to pack belongings from several different rooms in one box.
- Return library books and other loaned or borrowed items.
- Pick up clothing at the dry cleaner.
- Empty your safety deposit box at the bank.
- Place correct wires, components and literature in a labeled plastic bag and tape to or pack within the appliance.
- Pack remote controls with the correct electrical appliance or in designated and well-marked boxes.
- Color code cords and connectors to computers, stereos, VCRs and televisions for simplified reassembly.
- Set aside the vacuum cleaner and cleaning supplies.
- Clean and defrost the refrigerator/freezer.
- Clean all appliances that will remain in the house.

- Drain the washing machine.

*Note:* To prevent internal component damage to your television, turn it off 24 hours prior to moving. Then allow another 24 hours after plugging it in at the new home before turning it on. These time frames allow your electrical appliances to become adjusted to new temperature levels.

## ITEMS TO TAKE WITH YOU

Pack items that you may need as soon as you set foot in the new city, such as school and medical supplies, clothing appropriate for the season, important records and comfortable shoes.

SUGGESTIONS

- hotel telephone number and location
- destination moving company name and number
- shipping and storage documents
- personal addresses and telephone numbers
- jewelry/fur valuations
- camera and spare film
- a journal to record excerpts of your trip
- licenses
- personal and moving company household inventory
- keys for your new home
- outlet covers and night-lights for small children
- school records
- recommended list of doctors
- prescriptions for medications and inoculation records
- physician and dental records
- passports, visas and related documents
- airline tickets
- activities/games and books
- medical, auto and household goods insurance papers

# DEPARTURE DAY ESSENTIALS

Anything you can do to expedite your move and save time, labor and supplies equates to saving money. Just one of those chores is to collect items commonly needed on moving days in one trip, and then store them in a convenient location until moving day. Excess nonperishables should be packed in boxes marked "LAST ON."

### FOOD AND RELATED ITEMS

- food and beverages for moving day
- paper cups and bags with zipper closures
- paper plates/napkins/disposable utensils
- instant coffee/tea/milk/sugar

### ESSENTIALS

- aspirin/required medications
- first-aid kit
- paper towels/facial tissue/toilet tissue
- soap/disposable towelettes
- sewing kit
- car emergency equipment
- sunscreen and sunglasses
- travel alarm
- flashlight
- small tool kit
- large trash bags

### "THE KITCHEN DRAWER"

- scissors/pocketknife
- tape measure/collapsible ruler
- can opener/bottle opener/corkscrew

- paper/scratch pad/envelopes
- pen/pencil/marking pens
- cellophane tape/heavy-duty tape

## DEPARTURE DAY

- Clean and vacuum the house.
- Set the house temperature appropriately for the time of year.
- Turn off lights, appliances and ovens.
- Close and secure all windows.
- Leave a forwarding address and telephone number with a neighbor.
- Check closets, shelves, drawers to permanent cabinets, storage areas, the basement and the garage to be sure that everything has been packed.
- Give details such as telephone and fax numbers for your destination lodging to your moving company personnel so they can contact you upon arrival in the new location.
- Leave the garage door opener for the next owner.
- Lock your house.

# MOVING ON...

Before departing, confirm all your arrival and departure dates, flight numbers and routes to be sure nothing has changed since you made your reservations.

For airplane travel, pack jewelry and other valuables in your carry-on bag. If you need extra insurance for these items, you can ask the airline or your insurance agent.

If you are traveling by car, be aware of the varying state rules for auto lights, speed limits, safety concerns and emergency procedures. Detail your route on an easy-to-read map and review it with another passenger before you depart. Know the numbers to call for road assistance or emergencies and lock valuable items in the trunk.

### ITEMS TO PACK

- insurance and registration cards
- first aid kit
- spare set of car keys
- flare for emergencies, flashlight, whistle, battery jumper cables and a dependable spare tire
- extra clothing and blankets

## TRAVEL PRECAUTIONS

### SAFETY FOR SMALL CHILDREN

- Urge them to stay close to an adult in unfamiliar areas.
- Give them backup contact telephone numbers.
- Teach them their full names.
- Help them to learn and obey all traffic signals.
- Place a parent/guardian's business card or contact number inside their backpacks.
- Show them safe pedestrian procedures.

**SAFEGUARD YOUR MONEY**

- Don't carry extra credit cards.
- Don't be careless with your credit card receipts as account numbers can be copied and used.
- Take along credit card customer service telephone numbers.
- Traveler's checks will give you several purchase options.
- Carry your money separately from your identification.
- Make a list of your traveler's check numbers and keep it separate from the actual checks in case of loss.
- Photocopy your credit cards, identification and travel documents and keep them in a safe place.

*Note:* More financial advice appears in "BANK/FINANCE."

# MOVING IN

Your family may be living in temporary quarters until your belongings are delivered. Use this time to explore the new city as well as to establish home services, locate stores and find other family necessities. There are checklists of suggested home services and places to locate in the REFERENCE SECTION.

## YOUR NEW COMMUNITY

In the beginning of this book, I encouraged you to research the new city before you moved. Now that you have arrived, continue to learn everything you can about what the city has to offer. Use the pamphlets from your real estate agent and moving company and look for additional brochures, books and train/bus schedules at hotels and motels or the visitors' center.

Take your children on city excursions to help them become acclimated. Collect business cards everywhere you go so you can remember their services and locations. Also note the office hours and directions to these businesses on the back of the respective cards.

Medical care cannot be overemphasized. Accidents and illness often occur during a move, so if you have not already done so, locate hospitals, pharmacies and physicians that will meet your family's needs *as soon as possible*.

### GO EXPLORING

- Visit local historical museums and parks.
- Take a walking or bus tour of the city.
- Dine at restaurants which feature local cuisine.
- Acquaint your children with their schools and teachers and locate places where they will be spending their free time.
- Familiarize your family with the transportation services.

*See also* "FACT FINDING TRIP."

## SETTLING INTO A NEW HOME

Before the movers arrive, designate the different rooms in your home with numbers or names and display the room plans in the appropriate rooms. You will need one or more family members at the new residence when the moving truck arrives. If you have small children, try to make arrangements for their care during the move.

- Escort all the movers through the entire home and acquaint them with each room's furniture plan.

- Have someone available to note any dents or damages on the boxes or furniture.

- Keep pets on a leash, in a portable kennel or in a confined area. If your pet is easily excitable, consider boarding it or leaving it with a friend until the move is complete.

- Ask the movers to reassemble items such as beds and equipment that were taken apart at origin.

- Be sure to request the telephone numbers and names of firms that the moving company utilizes for reassembly of washers, dryers and other items.

One of the routines that we found extremely comforting in a new home was to establish a "box free" area early on. For us, the family room was the most practical and the easiest to set up. Concentrate on placing this furniture right away and save the job of filling shelves and cabinets for another day. The important point is to have one room in your new home that your family can enjoy as quickly as possible.

Give everyone a chore they can manage! Taking care of practical matters will take the edge off homesickness for everyone. Young children will feel better by unpacking boxes in their rooms and rediscovering treasures. The initial placement of these items does not have to be perfect; the important aspect is that the activity will be helpful to the children, as well as productive to you as more boxes are emptied. And consider treating yourselves to a casual dinner out the first night you are in the new home.

*Note:* Moving companies will usually pick up your used boxes.

Call them when you have emptied a substantial amount of containers.

## MAINTAINING CONTINUITY

From my own experience, I know that parents can feel guilty if their children are unhappy after a move. Parents realize that they are responsible for taking their children away from their comfortable environment and placing them in a situation where they have to "start all over," so to speak. I caution you not to allow these feelings to influence you when it comes to discipline or house rules. During the throes of a move, adults and children alike need the stability and comfort of established routines. You need to maintain the same rules, bed times, meal times, allowances and expectations for homework and chores that you had before you moved.

Stay abreast of your children's new school situations until you believe they are comfortably settled in. I suggest that you periodically visit school(s), meet with teachers and see for yourself how your children are managing. To learn more about how your children are adjusting, ask them questions that require specific answers, such as: What is your favorite class and why? Who have you met this week? What do you like best about your new home or your new city? Points that indicate children are not readily adjusting are listed in "Youth Corner."

Relocating to a new city or to a new region of your country can ultimately become an enriching experience for your family. Below are suggestions that have worked for many other relocating families and they can work for you as well. Hopefully the following suggestions will speed your transition and help you and your family become comfortable in your new home.

**TIPS TO SETTLE IN**

- √ *Learn something new about your community every week.*
- √ *Hold weekly family meetings to discuss problems and to share experiences that have occurred to each person in the past week. Encourage family members to discuss at least one positive episode during these meetings.*

- √ *Reach out to meet new people, such as joining groups with common interests such as athletic and special interest groups. (Community and religious organizations typically sponsor activities, volunteer efforts and programs for newcomers.)*
- √ *Share family stories and photos with each other and with new friends.*
- √ *Share your special family celebrations with new neighbors.*
- √ *Take one day at a time.*

## Note from BR Anchor Publishing

*The following REFERENCE SECTION has time-tested checklists that will help you quickly organize necessary relocation tasks.*

# REFERENCE SECTION

| | |
|---|---|
| SERVICES TO CANCEL | 78 |
| ADDRESS NOTIFICATION | 79 |
| ADDRESSES TO REMEMBER | 80 |
| PERSONAL INVENTORY | 81 |
| FAMILY RECORDS | 82 |
| FAMILY SUBSCRIPTIONS | 83 |
| CREDIT ACCOUNTS | 84 |
| INSURANCE | 85 |
| CURRENT PHYSICIANS | 86 - 87 |
| MEDICAL CHECKLIST | 88 |
| RETIREMENT CHECKLIST | 89 |
| ELDERCARE CHECKLIST | 90 |
| ELDERCARE EMERGENCY CHART | 91 |
| HOME SALE CHECKLISTS | 92 - 93 |
| SCHOOL REQUIREMENTS | 94 |
| SCHOOL FORM LETTER | 95 |
| PET/VETERINARIAN | 96 |
| LODGING/TRAVEL AND TRAVELER'S CHECKS | 97 |
| TRAVEL/HOME SAFETY | 98 |
| MOVING COMPANY/REAL ESTATE | 99 |
| NEW LOCATION | 100 |
| NEW SERVICES | 101 |
| HOME PURCHASE CHECKLISTS | 102 - 103 |
| HOME INSPECTIONS | 104 |
| NEW CONSTRUCTION/CONDOS | 105 |
| NEW PHYSICIANS | 106 |
| NEW HEALTH SERVICES/HOSPITAL | 107 |
| MILITARY CHECKLISTS | 108 - 110 |
| EMERGENCY CONTACTS | 111 |

Relocation 101

# SERVICES TO CANCEL

Contact your service providers in advance in case they require several weeks to cancel services. Retain electricity, telephone and heat services until the last day of packing. Request to have final statements and payments mailed to your new address.

**Check when contacted**                                       **Date**

- ☐ cable television     _____
- ☐ cell phone and Internet provider     _____
- ☐ city tax collector     _____
- ☐ electric     _____
- ☐ gas     _____
- ☐ local and long-distance telephone company     _____
- ☐ newspaper     _____
- ☐ oil     _____
- ☐ postal service     _____
- ☐ recycling company     _____
- ☐ refuse company     _____
- ☐ sewer     _____
- ☐ water     _____

other

- ☐ _____     _____
- ☐ _____     _____
- ☐ _____     _____
- ☐ _____     _____
- ☐ _____     _____
- ☐ _____     _____
- ☐ _____     _____

REFERENCE SECTION

# ADDRESS NOTIFICATION

Each time an invoice or publication comes through your mail slot, add it to the address notification list and keep it for your next move. Notify companies, organizations and the post office of your new address and move schedule.

**Check when contacted**                                    **Date**

- ☐ airline frequent flyer cards          _____
- ☐ bank                                  _____
- ☐ car registration                      _____
- ☐ college bursar's offices              _____
- ☐ company publication                   _____
- ☐ credit cards                          _____
- ☐ current driver's license              _____
- ☐ department stores                     _____
- ☐ finance/mortgage                      _____
- ☐ insurance companies                   _____
- ☐ Internal Revenue Service 1.800.829.3676   _____
- ☐ investments                           _____
- ☐ local personal accounts               _____
- ☐ magazines                             _____
- ☐ social security office                _____
- ☐ stocks/mutual funds                   _____
- ☐ voter registration                    _____

other

- ☐ _____        _____
- ☐ _____        _____
- ☐ _____        _____
- ☐ _____        _____

"ADDRESSES TO REMEMBER" is on the next page.

Relocation 101

# ADDRESSES TO REMEMBER

**Name/address** _____
_____
_____

Tel _____ E-mail _____

**Name/address** _____
_____
_____

Tel _____ E-mail _____

**Name/address** _____
_____
_____

Tel _____ E-mail _____

**Name/address** _____
_____
_____

Tel _____ E-mail _____

**Name/address** _____
_____
_____

Tel _____ E-mail _____

**Name/address** _____
_____
_____

Tel _____ E-mail _____

**Name/address** _____
_____
_____

Tel _____ E-mail _____

*Photocopy this page if you need more space.*

# PERSONAL INVENTORY

Document your household goods as recommended in "Relocation Insurance." This page may be photocopied.

| Article | Date | Value |
|---------|------|-------|
|         |      |       |
|         |      |       |
|         |      |       |
|         |      |       |
|         |      |       |
|         |      |       |
|         |      |       |
|         |      |       |
|         |      |       |
|         |      |       |
|         |      |       |
|         |      |       |
|         |      |       |
|         |      |       |
|         |      |       |
|         |      |       |
|         |      |       |
|         |      |       |
|         |      |       |
|         |      |       |
|         |      |       |
|         |      |       |
|         |      |       |
|         |      |       |
|         |      |       |

# FAMILY RECORDS

Update your important family records and carry necessities with you. Also consider guardianship arrangements for your children.

| Item | Location |
|---|---|
| **Family Records** | |
| birth certificates (original or certified) | _____ |
| divorce decree | _____ |
| guardianship | _____ |
| licenses | _____ |
| marriage certificate | _____ |
| medical files | _____ |
| passports | _____ |
| Power of Attorney | _____ |
| **Finances** | |
| stocks | _____ |
| tax returns | _____ |
| wills/estate planning | _____ |
| **Insurance** | |
| health | _____ |
| household | _____ |
| life | _____ |
| **Personal Property** | |
| auto titles | _____ |
| deed to home | _____ |
| household goods | _____ |
| video/inventory | _____ |
| jewelry/fur valuations | _____ |
| safety deposit box | _____ |
| **Other** | _____ |
| | _____ |

# FAMILY SUBSCRIPTIONS

**Publication** _____
Notification date _____

**Publication** _____
Notification date _____

**Publication** _____
Notification date _____

**Publication** _____
Notification date _____

**Publication** _____
Notification date _____

**Publication** _____
Notification date _____

**Publication** _____
Notification date _____

**Publication** _____
Notification date _____

**Publication** _____
Notification date _____

**Publication** _____
Notification date _____

**Publication** _____
Notification date _____

**Publication** _____
Notification date _____

# CREDIT ACCOUNTS

**Bank** _____
Account number _____
Contact _____
Tel _____ Date notified _____

**Bank** _____
Account number _____
Contact _____
Tel _____ Date notified _____

**Financial advisor** _____
Account number _____
Contact _____
Tel _____ Date notified _____

**Financial advisor** _____
Account number _____
Contact _____
Tel _____ Date notified _____

**Department store** _____
Account number _____
Contact _____
Tel _____ Date notified _____

**Department store** _____
Account number _____
Contact _____
Tel _____ Date notified _____

**Department store** _____
Account number _____
Contact _____
Tel _____ Date notified _____

# INSURANCE

**Carrier** _____
Policy no. _____ Plan _____
Contact _____
Tel _____ Claims _____
Date notified _____
Address _____

**Carrier** _____
Policy no. _____ Plan _____
Contact _____
Tel _____ Claims _____
Date notified _____
Address _____

**Carrier** _____
Policy no. _____ Plan _____
Contact _____
Tel _____ Claims _____
Date notified _____
Address _____

**Carrier** _____
Policy no. _____ Plan _____
Contact _____
Tel _____ Claims _____
Date notified _____
Address _____

Relocation 101

# CURRENT PHYSICIANS

Physician _____
**Family member** _____
Tel _____ Contact _____
Address _____
_____
Condition _____
Follow up _____

Physician _____
**Family member** _____
Tel _____ Contact _____
Address _____
_____
Condition _____
Follow up _____

Physician _____
**Family member** _____
Tel _____ Contact _____
Address _____
_____
Condition _____
Follow up _____

Physician _____
**Family member** _____
Tel _____ Contact _____
Address _____
_____
Condition _____
Follow up _____

# CURRENT PHYSICIANS

Physician _____
**Family member** _____
Tel _____ Contact _____
Address _____

Condition _____
Follow up _____


Physician _____
**Family member** _____
Tel _____ Contact _____
Address _____

Condition _____
Follow up _____


Physician _____
**Family member** _____
Tel _____ Contact _____
Address _____

Condition _____
Follow up _____


Physician _____
**Family member** _____
Tel _____ Contact _____
Address _____

Condition _____
Follow up _____

Relocation 101

# MEDICAL CHECKLIST

This checklist will complement the medical recommendations that were described in "New Medical Care."

- ☐ Pack your family's medical records that document illnesses, surgeries, broken bones and emergency ward visits.
- ☐ Take with you the addresses and telephone numbers of your current doctors, dentists and pharmacist.
- ☐ Take a supply of prescribed medications, plus original prescription forms to obtain refills.
- ☐ Keep all medications in their own labeled containers, noting the strength, dosage and prescribing physicians.
- ☐ Know the side effects of everyone's medications.
- ☐ Pack an anti-diarrhea medicine and an antibiotic if you are prone to severe infections when traveling.
- ☐ Take along your eye care prescriptions, as well as extra supplies to have until you are established with new services.
- ☐ Understand the procedure, telephone numbers and access codes to locate emergency care, i.e., the equivalent of 911.
- ☐ Know your alternatives if your medical plan will not be valid in the new city.
- ☐ Carry with you insurance forms and a medical ID card.

See also "Emergency Checklist" *in this section.*

Others

☐ _____
☐ _____
☐ _____
☐ _____
☐ _____
☐ _____

# RETIREMENT CHECKLIST

In the beginning of this book I mentioned a few points for relocating retirees. If you are among this group, here are more details to consider for your new community.

- ❒ cost of living, now and predictions for the future
- ❒ well-planned community, home and lot proximity
- ❒ convenient public transportation
- ❒ home and community assessments
- ❒ safe sidewalks and street traffic
- ❒ easy access for groceries, clothing and other necessities
- ❒ police, fire and emergency medical services (Are the services permanent or voluntary? Will they meet your needs?)
- ❒ cultural and sports activities

### Programs for seniors

If you want to work part-time to supplement your income, here are some resources you can check:

- ❒ senior centers, churches and the community;
- ❒ state or local offices of employment and aging;
- ❒ private companies that have specific programs for older workers (many utilize retired or semi-retired consultants on a part-time basis as opposed to keeping a permanently staffed employee);
- ❒ local colleges and technical schools;
- ❒ AARP's "Working Options" résumé and interviewing handbooks (see AARP's website in the INTERNET DIRECTORY).

Studies have shown that people who remain physically and mentally active live longer and happier lives. If you do not need financial compensation, think about volunteering for a charitable organization to help those in need in your community. Check your local newspaper, area churches and the Yellow Pages for suggestions.

# ELDERCARE CHECKLIST

**MAKING THE DECISION**
- ❏ Are we the only support system for our relative?
- ❏ Would he or she want to move with us?
- ❏ How would a move affect my relative's health?
- ❏ Would my relative adjust well to the new climate?
- ❏ What type of care, present and future, will be required? Is this care available in the new city?
- ❏ What resources (financial and personal) would be available if my relative remained in the same community?
- ❏ Is it possible that another move could follow this relocation?
- ❏ How will my relative's insurance and medical care be affected by relocation?
- ❏ What would the quality of life be like for my relative if he or she remained? What would it be like in the new city?

**FACILITY CONSIDERATIONS**
- ❏ How are the personnel screened?
- ❏ What is the proximity of transportation, shopping and places of worship?
- ❏ Is it handicap accessible?
- ❏ Are residents permitted to use their own furniture and personal belongings?
- ❏ Are the other residents pleased with their accommodations?
- ❏ Is the staff or facility licensed and accredited?
- ❏ Will nurses or therapists evaluate the patient's needs?
- ❏ Will my family be included in developing a plan of care?
- ❏ Do you assign supervisors to oversee the quality of care patients are receiving? If so, how often?
- ❏ Who can our family call with questions or complaints?
- ❏ What are the financial terms and procedures?
- ❏ How are problems resolved?

REFERENCE SECTION

# ELDERCARE EMERGENCY CHART

Full name _____
Address _____
_____

Telephone _____
Date of birth _____
Social Security number _____
Medicare health insurance policy number _____
Allergies _____
Blood type _____
Current medications (name and purpose) _____
_____

Learn the 911 equivalent for ambulance, fire and police emergencies.

| **HEALTH CARE** | **NETWORK** |
|---|---|
| Doctor _____ | Family _____ |
| Doctor _____ | Family _____ |
| Dentist _____ | Family _____ |
| Hospital _____ | Neighbor _____ |
| 24 hr. pharmacy _____ | Neighbor _____ |
| Aging agency _____ | Friend _____ |
| Nursing agency _____ | Friend _____ |
| Health insurance _____ | Senior center _____ |
| _____ | Social worker _____ |
| _____ | Clergy _____ |
| _____ | Church group _____ |
| _____ | Co-worker _____ |

**SERVICES**

| | |
|---|---|
| Electrician _____ | Landlord _____ |
| Electric Co. _____ | Banker _____ |
| Water Co. _____ | Attorney _____ |
| Gas Co. _____ | Accountant _____ |
| TV cable _____ | Insurance agent _____ |
| Plumber _____ | House alarm _____ |
| Home care _____ | Locksmith _____ |
| House sitter _____ | Pet sitter _____ |

© Copyright *The Complete Eldercare Planner.* Reprinted with permission.

# HOME SALE CHECKLIST

### OUTSIDE—THE FIRST IMPRESSION

Critique your home as though you were seeing it through a buyer's eyes. If it has been awhile since you made additions or upgrades to your property and you believe it needs a little help, a facelift can make a huge difference. Here are points to check so that when potential buyers drive by your home, they will want to make an appointment to see it.

- ❒ Prune and fertilize lawns, shrubs and trees.
- ❒ Add flowers, especially around prominent areas, such as the front walks and entryway.
- ❒ Store all bicycles, toys and garden tools, making the outside as neat as the inside of your home.
- ❒ Make house numbers clearly visible.
- ❒ Store unattractive items such as trash cans out of site.
- ❒ Clean, repair and/or paint:
    - front, side and back of the house, plus paths and patios;
    - windows, sills, doors, garage doors, shutters and screens;
    - paths and patios;
    - mailbox and flower boxes.
- ❒ All mechanical items that stay with the house, such as the garage door openers, should be in good working order.

Finally, look at other homes in your neighborhood. Be sure your home shows at least as well as, and preferably better than, comparable homes.

REFERENCE SECTION

# HOME SALE CHECKLIST

**INSIDE—MAKE IT COUNT**

Prepare your home for showings by creating a salable atmosphere and have as few family members present as possible. Play soft music, provide lots of lighting (even in the daytime), open drapery and blinds, remove pets and set the thermostat to a comfortable temperature. Additional points to note:

- ❐ Maintain a fresh environment. If your carpet has unpleasant odors, sprinkle baking soda on the carpet, let it stand for 15 minutes and then vacuum.
- ❐ Put clean towels in bathrooms.
- ❐ Create an orderly appearance everywhere in your home. Consider bathrooms, closets, basements, attics and kitchen counters (limit the number of countertop appliances).
- ❐ Clean all appliances that remain with the home and provide appropriate literature for these appliances.
- ❐ Organize closets, diminish excess items and hang clothing neatly.
- ❐ Tighten hinges and knobs.
- ❐ Clear all stairways.
- ❐ Repair leaky faucets.
- ❐ Clean windows, walls and woodwork.
- ❐ Replace or refurbish any out-of-date or mismatched appliances or cabinetry if possible.
- ❐ Keep your home ready to be shown *at all times*. House-hunters are usually in town for short periods of time. Therefore, it is not unusual to have a real estate agent call and say: "We must see your home in the next hour!"

Painting is the number one improvement to consider, both inside and outside. The expense, which is relatively low, is a good investment. If you are pressed for time or money to paint, at least be sure that all areas are clean.

Relocation 101

# SCHOOL REQUIREMENTS

Child's name _____

**Current school** _____

Years in attendance _____

Address _____
_____

Contact _____ Tel _____

**Records to Pack**     **Comments**

❒ achievement tests _____

❒ medical history _____

❒ transcripts _____

❒ other _____

Academic level _____

Textbooks _____  _____
         _____  _____
         _____  _____

**New school** _____

Address _____
_____

Contact _____ Tel _____

**Records Required**     **Comments**

❒ achievement tests _____

❒ medical history _____

❒ transcripts _____

❒ other _____

❒ _____

*Photocopy this page if you need more space.*

# SCHOOL FORM LETTER

Consider the following suggestions when inquiring about prospective schools. You can use the form letter or refer to the questions when calling schools. Add specifics that are unique to your situation. It is helpful to enclose a self-addressed, stamped envelope (SASE) and telephone and fax numbers for responses. You will find more areas to consider in "Evaluating New Schools."

Date
Principal name
School name
School Address
City, State ZIP

Dear          :

Due to our family's new assignment, we will be relocating to {name of city} on {date of move}. We have {number} children, {names and ages}. We would appreciate it if you could respond to the following questions to help us make an informed decision.

1   What safety policies are enforced at your school?
2   What courses of study are available (honors level, vocational, electives)?
3   What are the school hours?
4   What is the school's annual operation calendar?
5   What are the enrollment requirements?
6   Can scholarship credentials be transferred to your school?
7   What percentage of your high school graduates enroll in college?
8   Are parent/teacher organizations active?
9   What courses are required for graduation?
10  Is technology utilized and encouraged?
11  What extracurricular activities are available?
12  What percentage of your students are military dependents?
13  Does your school or district have a website?

Please send us information regarding these points in the enclosed SASE, fax information to {fax number} or call me at {phone number}. We look forward to hearing from you at your earliest convenience.

Sincerely,

{Sign and type your name}

Relocation 101

# PET/VETERINARIAN

**Name of pet** _____

Species _____ Male _____ Female _____

License # _____

Color markings _____

_____

**Owner** _____

Tel # 1 _____ # 2 _____

Address _____

_____

**Acquire an identification tag with the new address.**

Veterinarian _____

Address _____

_____

Tel/Fax _____

Emergency information _____

| **Vaccination/Appointments** | **Date** |
|---|---|
| _____ | _____ |
| _____ | _____ |
| _____ | _____ |
| _____ | _____ |

| **Condition/Illness** | **Treatment/Medication** |
|---|---|
| _____ | _____ |
| _____ | _____ |
| _____ | _____ |

Schedule a health examination for your pet before you move. To locate a new veterinarian, contact the American Animal Hospital Association (AAHA) at 1.800.883.6301.

Copyright © BR Anchor Publishing

# LODGING/TRAVEL

**Hotel** _____
Tel _____ Fax _____
E-mail address _____
Date of arrival _____
Date of departure _____
Address _____
_____

Directions/other information _____
_____
_____
_____

# TRAVELER'S CHECKS

**Banking source** _____
Check nos. from _____ to _____
Currency _____
Denomination _____
Number to call for questions or loss _____
Checks in the name of _____

**Banking source** _____
Checks from _____ to _____
Currency _____
Denomination _____
Number to call for questions or loss _____
Checks in the name of _____

Keep records of all travel expenses with amounts, dates and relevant information regarding the expense. *See also* "BANK/FINANCE."

# TRAVEL SAFETY

- ❏ Before leaving home, inform an extended family member of your travel plans, route of travel and how to contact you.
- ❏ Have everyone in the family carry personal identification.
- ❏ Children should know their own name, their parents' names, telephone numbers and who they can contact in case of an emergency.
- ❏ Wear a travel bag strapped to your waist to conceal personal papers and money.
- ❏ Use well-traveled routes in new cities.
- ❏ Learn the city's rules, regulations, curfews and safe streets.
- ❏ Keep a low profile and remain alert in unfamiliar places.

# HOME SAFETY

- ❏ Install new locks on a previously owned home or rental property and use deadbolt locks on all exterior doors.
- ❏ Always use the alarm system when the family is absent from the home.
- ❏ Plan one or two exit routes for your family in case of fire.
- ❏ Place a locking bar on all sliding glass doors.
- ❏ Secure all ladders.
- ❏ Tell trusted neighbors and police when you are on vacation.
- ❏ Do not hide keys outside of your home.
- ❏ Check smoke detector batteries twice a year.
- ❏ Discontinue mail and newspaper deliveries when traveling.
- ❏ Install night lights, sensor lights and timers inside and outside the home. Keep flashlights accessible.
- ❏ Use baby gates and child-resistant locks.
- ❏ Purchase a fire extinguisher for your home.
- ❏ Ask a neighbor to periodically check on your home, turn lights on and off and give your home a "lived in" look.

*See also* "EMERGENCY CONTACTS" *in this section.*

# MOVING COMPANY

**Origination company** _____
Agent _____
Address _____
Tel _____ Fax _____
Moving dates _____
E-mail _____ Website _____

**Destination company** _____
Contact _____
Anticipated arrival date of goods _____
Tel _____ Fax _____
Details _____
E-mail _____ Website _____

# REAL ESTATE

**Origination company** _____
Agent _____
Address _____

Tel _____ Fax _____
Details _____

E-mail _____ Website _____

**Destination company** _____
Agent _____
Address _____

Tel _____ Fax _____
Details _____
E-mail _____ Website _____

# NEW LOCATION

**SIGNIFICANT AREAS TO LOCATE**
- ❒ the nearest hospital _____
- ❒ fire/police departments _____

- ❒ pharmacy _____
- ❒ place of worship _____
- ❒ convenient bank branch _____
- ❒ beauty/barber shops _____

- ❒ transportation service _____
- ❒ school and bus stop _____

- ❒ doctors' and dentists' offices (*See also* "NEW MEDICAL CARE")
- ❒ veterinary office/pet hospital _____

- ❒ pet food/supplies _____
- ❒ plumber/repair services _____

- ❒ dry cleaner _____
- ❒ shopping centers _____

- ❒ market _____
- ❒ restaurants _____

other _____

REFERENCE SECTION

# NEW SERVICES

Your real estate agent or landlord can help you to locate new utility and household services. Establish these services before you move in, especially the electricity, telephone and heat. This is the time to request additional telephone, cable, fax and Internet access jacks.

**Notified**                                                    **Date**

- ❐ cable television                                            _____
- ❐ cell phone and Internet provider                            _____
- ❐ city tax collector                                          _____
- ❐ electric                                                    _____
- ❐ gas                                                         _____
- ❐ local and long-distance telephone company                   _____
- ❐ newspaper                                                   _____
- ❐ oil                                                         _____
- ❐ postal service                                              _____
- ❐ recycling company                                           _____
- ❐ refuse company                                              _____
- ❐ sewer                                                       _____
- ❐ water                                                       _____

other

- ❐ _____  _____
- ❐ _____  _____
- ❐ _____  _____
- ❐ _____  _____
- ❐ _____  _____
- ❐ _____  _____
- ❐ _____  _____

Copyright © BR Anchor Publishing

Relocation 101

# HOME PURCHASE CHECKLIST

**ADDRESS** _____

## Community

|  | Excellent | Good | Fair |
|---|---|---|---|
| progressive school system | ☐ | ☐ | ☐ |
| neighborhood/development | ☐ | ☐ | ☐ |
| police, fire and emergency medical service | ☐ | ☐ | ☐ |
| surrounding properties and views | ☐ | ☐ | ☐ |
| sidewalks for busy streets | ☐ | ☐ | ☐ |
| trash and garbage disposal | ☐ | ☐ | ☐ |
| public transportation | ☐ | ☐ | ☐ |
| other _____ | ☐ | ☐ | ☐ |

## Home

|  | Excellent | Good | Fair |
|---|---|---|---|
| square footage | ☐ | ☐ | ☐ |
| sunny and comfortable rooms | ☐ | ☐ | ☐ |
| walls, floors and carpentry | ☐ | ☐ | ☐ |
| bedroom privacy from the living area | ☐ | ☐ | ☐ |
| lighting and ventilation in the kitchen | ☐ | ☐ | ☐ |
| kitchen outlets, cabinets and counter space | ☐ | ☐ | ☐ |
| closets and storage areas | ☐ | ☐ | ☐ |
| electrical, heating and cooling systems | ☐ | ☐ | ☐ |
| garage or carport | ☐ | ☐ | ☐ |
| doors, windows and drawers | ☐ | ☐ | ☐ |
| plumbing | ☐ | ☐ | ☐ |
| stairs and handrail convenience | ☐ | ☐ | ☐ |
| landscaping | ☐ | ☐ | ☐ |
| water source and water pressure | ☐ | ☐ | ☐ |
| roof gutters and downspouts | ☐ | ☐ | ☐ |
| overall energy efficiency | ☐ | ☐ | ☐ |
| other _____ | ☐ | ☐ | ☐ |
| _____ | ☐ | ☐ | ☐ |
| _____ | ☐ | ☐ | ☐ |

Copyright © BR Anchor Publishing

REFERENCE SECTION

# HOME PURCHASE CHECKLIST

**ADDRESS** _____

| **Community** | Excellent | Good | Fair |
|---|---|---|---|
| progressive school system | ☐ | ☐ | ☐ |
| neighborhood/development | ☐ | ☐ | ☐ |
| police, fire and emergency medical service | ☐ | ☐ | ☐ |
| surrounding properties and views | ☐ | ☐ | ☐ |
| sidewalks for busy streets | ☐ | ☐ | ☐ |
| trash and garbage disposal | ☐ | ☐ | ☐ |
| public transportation | ☐ | ☐ | ☐ |
| other _____ | ☐ | ☐ | ☐ |

| **Home** | Excellent | Good | Fair |
|---|---|---|---|
| square footage | ☐ | ☐ | ☐ |
| sunny and comfortable rooms | ☐ | ☐ | ☐ |
| walls, floors and carpentry | ☐ | ☐ | ☐ |
| bedroom privacy from the living area | ☐ | ☐ | ☐ |
| lighting and ventilation in the kitchen | ☐ | ☐ | ☐ |
| kitchen outlets, cabinets and counter space | ☐ | ☐ | ☐ |
| closets and storage areas | ☐ | ☐ | ☐ |
| electrical, heating and cooling systems | ☐ | ☐ | ☐ |
| garage or carport | ☐ | ☐ | ☐ |
| doors, windows and drawers | ☐ | ☐ | ☐ |
| plumbing | ☐ | ☐ | ☐ |
| stairs and handrail convenience | ☐ | ☐ | ☐ |
| landscaping | ☐ | ☐ | ☐ |
| water source and water pressure | ☐ | ☐ | ☐ |
| roof gutters and downspouts | ☐ | ☐ | ☐ |
| overall energy efficiency | ☐ | ☐ | ☐ |
| other _____ | ☐ | ☐ | ☐ |
| _____ | ☐ | ☐ | ☐ |
| _____ | ☐ | ☐ | ☐ |

Copyright © BR Anchor Publishing

# HOME INSPECTIONS

Following is a sample of home features that are usually inspected. Others may be added depending on the age and type of the home, its location and the company that performs the service.

- ❏ heating and cooling systems (age, condition and operation)
- ❏ fireplace, flue, chimney and thermostat(s)
- ❏ electrical systems (amperage and light switches, door bells and outside lights)
- ❏ insulation
- ❏ plumbing, water heater, commodes, showers, drains, tiling and faucets
- ❏ major appliances that are sold with the home such as the oven, stove, dishwasher, refrigerator/freezer, garbage disposal, washer and dryer (and drains)
- ❏ walls throughout the home, basement, attic, crawl spaces, garage, floors and ceiling (cracking, mildew and water stains)
- ❏ radon, lead and asbestos testing
- ❏ kitchen cabinetry and counters
- ❏ roof, siding, windows and doors, steps, decks, porches, foundation and landscaping
- ❏ mechanical systems

**RESOURCES:**

Check the Yellow Pages of your telephone directory under "Engineers—Consulting" or "Building Inspection Services."

The American Society of Home Inspectors (ASHI) is a not-for-profit organization to build awareness of home inspection and to enhance the technical and professional performance of home inspectors. To locate an inspector nearest you, call 1.800.743.2744.

# NEW CONSTRUCTION/CONDOS

**CONSTRUCTION POINTS TO CONSIDER**
- ❐ quality interior and exterior materials
- ❐ excellent plumbing and fixtures
- ❐ hardwood flooring
- ❐ large unique windows
- ❐ spacious master bedroom
- ❐ large organized closets
- ❐ large kitchen with a convenient layout and good cabinetry
- ❐ security systems
- ❐ fire alarm and smoke detectors
- ❐ high ceilings
- ❐ convenient floor plan
- ❐ attractive front door and ample foyer
- ❐ well-designed landscaping

**CONDOMINIUM CONSIDERATIONS**
- ❐ Many condominiums have interior space that is similar to single-family homes.
- ❐ You will not be responsible for outside maintenance, lawn care or snow removal.
- ❐ Homeowner dues are typically applied toward club houses and/or pools.
- ❐ Owners are sometimes limited in the colors, types and amount of exterior and interior decorations they can use, as well as the amount of renovations they can make.
- ❐ Close proximity to neighbors can result in excess noise levels and less privacy.
- ❐ Owners are dependent on the Homeowners Association for unit repairs.
- ❐ Check the outside lighting for walkways and parking lots, plus review the points mentioned in "HOME PURCHASES."

Relocation 101

# NEW PHYSICIANS

Physician _____
**Family member** _____
Tel _____ Contact _____
Address _____

Condition _____
Follow up _____

Physician _____
**Family member** _____
Tel _____ Contact _____
Address _____

Condition _____
Follow up _____

Physician _____
**Family member** _____
Tel _____ Contact _____
Address _____

Condition _____
Follow up _____

Physician _____
**Family member** _____
Tel _____ Contact _____
Address _____

Condition _____
Follow up _____

*Photocopy this page if you need more space.*

# NEW HEALTH SERVICES

Physician-patient compatibility is as important as the quality of service you receive. Take the time to meet with prospective doctors and dentists before an accident or illness occurs.

### NEW PHYSICIAN SERVICES
- ❐ references from reliable sources
- ❐ accessibility of the office
- ❐ diversity of care
- ❐ accepted insurance
- ❐ terms, conditions and method of payment if insurance is not accepted
- ❐ qualifications of the physicians
- ❐ hours of availability
- ❐ back-up care in case of an emergency
- ❐ hospitals with which the physicians are affiliated

*See also* "MEDICAL" *in the* INTERNET DIRECTORY.

Personal preferences
_____
_____

# NEW HOSPITAL

Name _____

Tel _____ Contact _____

Address _____
_____

Directions _____
_____

Notes _____
_____

RELOCATION 101

# MILITARY CHECKLIST

These checklists provide an overview for military families in addition to the other checklists in this book. Visit your relocation office and check the military websites in the INTERNET DIRECTORY for comprehensive information about your new base.

**BEFORE YOU MOVE**

- ❒ After receiving your official PCS/travel orders, review base housing cleaning instructions, arrange for your house to be cleaned again in case you fail inspection and do not have the time to redo it yourself. Schedule a final walk through. Remember to make arrangements for lawn care.
- ❒ Call two weeks prior to your departure to set up an appointment for your final out-processing.
- ❒ Make an appointment with the appropriate office(s) to receive travel tickets and arrange for shipment of your household goods.
- ❒ Pick up a Family Member Clearance Package.
- ❒ Call your current Family Center for information about the new installation. Be sure you have a list of all your family's needs/questions to ask the family support consultant. Also inquire about lodging and/or airplane reservations or any specific procedures and obtain relevant telephone numbers and e-mail addresses. Check DoD installations via the Internet sites listed under "MILITARY" in the INTERNET DIRECTORY.
- ❒ Evaluate your "express" or "hold baggage" shipment and what you will need for light housekeeping until your surface shipment arrives (frequently several weeks).
- ❒ Leave the telephone plugged in until you are ready to depart, then pack it and a telephone book in your express shipment.
- ❒ Attend your base finance out-processing and any relocation briefings.
- ❒ Give your extended family the telephone number of the Red Cross so they can notify you immediately in the event of serious illness or death in the family. This also speeds the authorization process for emergency leave.

# MILITARY CHECKLIST

- ❒ If you have a cell phone and e-mail, make sure everyone who may need to contact you has this information.
- ❒ Weigh military books, papers and equipment independently. These items will be listed on the shipping inventory and then packed apart from your other goods.
- ❒ Single parents/dual career military couples with children should update the Dependent Care Certificate (OPNAV17 40/1), available at local Personnel Support Detachments. This certificate allows a designated adult to care for your children in your absence. Marine families should contact their S-1 (Administrative Office).
- ❒ Ensure that your immediate family members are properly listed on the Defense Eligibility Enrollment Reporting System (DEERS).
- ❒ Check with the personnel office to renew ID cards that will be expiring.
- ❒ Arrange for appropriate care and transportation of your family pet. There is a pet checklist in the REFERENCE SECTION and pet websites listed in the INTERNET DIRECTORY.
- ❒ Contact your sponsor or command for departure information, enroute stops, carrier, arrival date/time and number of family members accompanying you.
- ❒ Working spouses should check with their Family Center for help with résumés and job search before and after their moves.
- ❒ Order "Moving Publication" #521 from the Internal Revenue Service to take advantage of current military deductions. Forms are available at post offices or through the IRS at www.irs.gov or 1.800.829.3676.

*Note:* The Exceptional Family Member (EFM) Program benefits service families that require long-term health care or special education. It assists service members in providing for the needs of their EFM before, during and after a relocation required by change of duty assignments. The program confirms the availability of special medical and educational resources near major medical facilities.

# MILITARY CHECKLIST

### Carry with you

- ❐ Required uniforms for inprocessing (or pack so they are easily accessible)
- ❐ Proof of family members from your service record
- ❐ Military ID cards for all family members 10 years of age and older (check expiration dates to be sure they will remain valid throughout the move)
- ❐ A Power of Attorney or Letter of Authorization, notarized or countersigned by the base Legal Office
- ❐ Registration for any motorized vehicle, motorcycle, boat or trailer to be shipped
- ❐ The make, caliber and serial number of firearms being shipped
- ❐ Number to Tricare (in case of a medical emergency)

Other recommended documents include: Area Clearance papers, Original Orders and a spouse's résumé if doing active duty part-time civilian work. Also refer to "ITEMS TO TAKE WITH YOU," "FAMILY RECORDS" and other travel checklists throughout this book.

### Arrival checklist

- ❐ Contact the base authority at the new duty station as soon as possible upon arrival. Give the office a contact telephone number.
- ❐ Arrange for delivery of personal property through your Transportation Management Office (TMO).
- ❐ Following delivery, list all damages and missing items on the proper form, and ensure that the correct number of copies are given to the moving company to record loss or damage. Keep the copy of your Claim sheet in case there is loss or damage.

# EMERGENCY CONTACTS

In an emergency, you may forget your new telephone number and/or address. Before an emergency arises, write down basic directions to your home on this page and keep a copy of it near each telephone in your home.

**Contact**                                                **Telephone number**

- ❏ emergency    _____
- ❏ fire    _____
- ❏ ambulance    _____
- ❏ police    _____
- ❏ poison center    _____
- ❏ operator    _____
- ❏ weather    _____
- ❏ work    _____
- ❏ neighbor    _____
- ❏ other    _____

**Directions to your home**

_____
_____
_____
_____

**Family allergies or other concerns**

_____
_____
_____
_____

# INTERNET DIRECTORY

### Note from BR Anchor Publishing

*The Internet sites listed in this book were reviewed by our staff for content and found to be helpful resources for our readers. Although all sites were accurate at the time this book went to press, websites are subject to change without notice.*

## TRAVEL AND SAFETY

**Centers for Disease Control and Prevention** www.cdc.gov

**Priceline.com** www.priceline.com Name Your Own Price...and Save!

**The Weather Channel** www.weather.com Find weather conditions in your new city and around the world.

**TripSpot** www.tripspot.com Access low airfares, hotels, car rentals and any other travel service you might require.

## MEDICAL

**American Medical Association** (AMA) www.ama-assn.org
The Doctor Finder, Consumer Health Information and National Patient Safety Foundation (NPSF).

**DoctorDirectory.com** www.doctordirectory.com A comprehensive user-friendly resource for finding the right physician.

**Visiting Nurse Associations of America** (VNAA) www.vnaa.com At the heart of home health care.

**WebMD** www.webmd.com Provides services that help physicians, consumers, providers and health plans navigate the complexity of the healthcare system.

## REAL ESTATE

**Apartments.com** www.apartments.com A national apartment guide and relocation resource with customized searches, visual ads and affiliation with more than 150 newspapers across the country.

**EBASearch.com** www.ebasearch.com Find A Buyer's Agent no matter where you live, get help through their For Sale By Owner link or obtain a free copy of your credit report.

**Fannie Mae** www.fanniemae.com Helps low- to middle-income families achieve the American dream of home ownership.

**FiSBO Registry, Inc.** www.fisbos.com A full range of choices for your real estate marketing whether you are buying or selling. Specializing in For Sale By Owner (FSBO) transactions.

**HomeSteps** www.homesteps.com A variety of value-priced properties all across America. Many are refurbished to like-new condition.

**HomeStore.com** www.homestore.com/apartments Photos, floor plans and virtual tours of apartments and rentals in the US and Canada.

## REAL ESTATE Continued

**Homes.wsj.com** www.homes.wsj.com Locate property, research a new city, plan a relocation or track down the sales history of a particular home just by typing in its address.

**Relocation Scout** www.relocationscout.com Real Estate Agents, city searches, rentals, mortgage firms, financing, home warranties, moving and storage firms and more.

## DUAL CAREER RESOURCES

**America's Career InfoNet** www.acinet.org Wages and employment trends, state by state labor market, employer contacts and an extensive career resource library.

**Careerbuilder** www.careerbuilder.com Classifieds from major newspapers and résumé and employer/job matching services.

**Career Journal** www.careerjournal.com The premier career site for executives, managers and professionals.

**International Staffing Consultants, Inc.** www.iscworld.com Recruits and selects professionals/technicians.

**JobOptions** www.joboptions.com Perform a job search, post your résumé, sign up for e-mail job alerts and compare your salary.

**Monster.com** www.monster.com Offers free résumé hosting, job postings, career advice and salary information.

**Options/Resource Careers, Inc.** www.optionsrc.com Provides dual career job search assistance and destination services worldwide. Partnerships with corporate clients ensure cost-effective services tailored to meet individual needs through a centralized account management team and community-based service providers in 200+ cities throughout 50 countries.

**Ricklin-Echikson Associates, Inc.** www.r-e-a.com Specializing in employment assistance for spouses/partners of relocated employees, career counseling and outplacement services worldwide.

### TEMPORARY WORK SITES

**Kelly Services** www.kellyservices.com Provides innovative and effective staffing solutions which are tailored to meet individual business needs.

**Manpower** www.manpower.com  Helps customers manage their human resources more effectively. Innovative technologies and creative solutions.

## VOLUNTEER SITES

**Advice for Volunteers** www.serviceleader.org/advice  Advice to choose, maximize, set boundaries and develop expectations regarding volunteerism. Includes an index of links to volunteer websites.

**Girl Scouts of the USA** www.girlscouts.org  Click on Adults in Girl Scouting to learn about employment opportunities, volunteer resources and online training.

**Idea List** www.idealist.org  Lists over 20,000 organizations in 150 countries. Programs, services, guides, internships and an ezine.

# EDUCATION

**American School Directory** www.asd.com  A subscription based site with accurate and timely information on K-12 schools throughout the US.

**Bennett Educational Resources, Inc. (BER)** www.schoolplacement.com. Specialists in school and college/university selection and placement support to relocating families. BER publishes *"Factors to Consider When Selecting a School."*

**Homeschool World** www.home-school.com  Articles, homeschool organizations and events, shop at Homeschool Mall and more.

**Home Schooling Central** www.HSLDA.org  Home School Legal Defense Association provides selected news and announcements, statistics and reports and access to state home schooling laws.

**Ivy West Educational Services, Inc.** www.ivywest.com  Personalized preparation for SAT and other standardized tests. Information about testing, college admissions and academic resources.

**Schools.com** www.schools.com  An independent non-profit educational organization exclusively serving boarding schools and students based in the US.

**US Department of Education** www.ed.gov/offices  Award winning site designed for parents and administrators to ensure equal access to education, and to promote educational excellence.

## CHILD CARE

**Careguide** www.careguide.com  Search for child care or elder care anywhere in the United States and access multiple resources.

**National Association of Child Care Resource and Referral Agencies** www.naccrra.net  Find the child care Resource and Referral agency (R&R) that serves your area. The site also has a Professional Opportunities section with jobs for child care professionals.

## FINANCES

**Internal Revenue Service** of the US Department of Treasury www.irs.ustreas.gov

**JobStar** www.jobstar.org/tools/salary  Over 300 salary surveys, plus negotiation strategies, career guides and résumé assistance.

**Money Magazine** www.money.com  Includes a host of money oriented services, e-mail newsletters, stocks, mortgages and much more.

**WageWeb** www.wageweb.com  Salary survey data and benchmark positions with compensation data.

## MILITARY ASSISTANCE

**Air Force Crossroads** www.afcrossroads.com  Links to resources, installations, spouse networks, employment opportunities and more.

**MarineLINK** www.usmc.mil  Wide range of information. Marine Corps opportunities, public events, fact files, history and publications.

**Military Assistance Program (MAP)** www.dod.mil/mapsite  The Relocation Station, the Money Station and the Employment Station for all military personnel.

**Militarylifestyle.com** http://www.militarylifestyle.com  Editorial content is updated daily—features, news, personality profiles, retirement and benefits coverage, etc.

**Military OncSource** www.militaryonesource.com  Whether it is help with child care, personal finances, emotional support during deployments, relocation information or resources needed for special circumstances, we are here... 24/7/365!

**TRICARE Military Health Site** www.tricare.osd.mil Medical Management, DentalWare Management, medical statement processing and a host of other services.

**U.S. Army** www.army.mil Includes army alumni association database, personnel locator and a center for military history.

**U.S. Coast Guard** www.uscg.mil Check FAQ, the images and facts section and find unit locations. Career and educational opportunities.

**U.S. Navy** www.navy.mil Resources, links to naval-related websites, the naval public affairs library and Lifelines.

## ELDER CARE

**Elder Care Workshop** www.elderindustry.com *The Complete Eldercare Planner* and work/life presentations by Joy Loverde.

**ElderCare Online** www.ec-online.net Whether you are caring for a spouse, parent, relative or neighbor, ElderCare Online is committed to providing an online community where supportive peers and professionals help you improve quality of life for yourself and your elder.

**The National Academy of Elder Law Attorneys, Inc.** www.naela.com NEALA is a non-profit association that assists lawyers, bar organizations and others who work with older clients and their families.

**Transitions, Inc.** www.asktransitions.com Light-hearted and fun site to educate and support those touched by the aging process. Assistance to individuals and employers available.

*See also* "CAREGUIDE" *under* CHILD CARE

## RELOCATION MANAGEMENT

**National Equity** www.neirelo.com A full-service relocation management company, providing an array of origination, destination and administrative services domestically and internationally.

**Relocation Property Services** (RPS) www.rpsrelocation.com Certified relocation service providers that offer discount services.

**Selection Research International** (SRI) www.sri-2000.com Focusing on job performance and family adaptation to increase the effectiveness of assignment management.

## RETIREMENT

**American Association of Retired Persons (AARP)**  www.aarp.org
Health, wellness, legislative issues, life transitions, money and work.

**Best Retirement Spots** www.bestretirementspots.com  Vacation rentals, real estate and retirement communities, great links for seniors, legal advice and more.

**The Retirement Net Online**  www.retirenet.com  Browse through the category that best describes your lifestyle, or be as specific as you want with their powerful Community Search.

## OTHER RELEVANT SITES

**Grandparent Support Group**
www.aarp.org/grandparents  For grandparents raising grandchildren and grandparents from a distance. Safety tips, insurance advice and support to find programs in your community.

**Parents Without Partners, Incorporated**  www.parentswithoutpartners.org  Providing education, recreation, social services and activities to single parents and their children.

**Maps.com**  www.maps.com  Your one stop shop for maps. Driving directions within the USA, as well as world maps.

**MovingCenter**  www.movingcenter.com  Community information, apartments, real estate, moving services and post-move tips.

**Moving.com**  www.moving.com  Select a moving or truck rental company, locate a real estate agent, obtain a copy of your credit report and change your address with the U.S. Post Office.

**Newspaper Links**  www.newspaperlinks.com  Daily, weekly, international, college, associations and newspaper archives.

**Service Corps of Retired Executives (SCORE)**  www.score.org  Providing entrepreneurs with free, confidential face-to-face and e-mail business counseling and workshops.

**The List**  thelist.internet.com  Find an Internet Service Provider (ISP).

## PETS

**Healthypet's Hospital Locator** www.healthypet.com  Use Healthypet's Hospital Locator to find a veterinary hospital near you or nearly anywhere you want to go.

**Jet-A-Pet** www.jet-a-pet.com  Provides domestic and international pet, dog and animal transportation and travel services.

# MORE SITES...

# ABOUT THE AUTHOR

Beverly D. Roman has written more than thirty domestic and international relocation books and published the international newsletter, *Relocation Today* for over 15 years. The author is recognized and quoted as an expert in the field of relocation. Having relocated 19 times with a family of five, Beverly has a thorough understanding of what is productive and what is counterproductive to achieving relocation success.

Beverly has been featured on radio shows such as Army Wife Talk Radio, and appeared on CNN, ABC and Discovery Channel television networks. She has written for industry magazines including *Runzheimer Reports on Relocation*, *Mobility*, *Personnel Journal*, *Direction*, *Horizons*, *HR Briefing*, numerous parents' magazines and *The Weekly Telegraph*, London, England. Beverly was sourced among such distinguished organizations as Employee Relocation Council and Runzheimer International in *Developing An International Relocation Policy That's Right For Your Company* for American Red Ball World Wide Movers. The author was also among the thought leaders chosen to write what she perceived to be the most critical relocation challenges for 2005 for Human Resource Executive's annual Forecast issue.

Beverly served as Chairperson for Families in Global Transition, Inc. (FIGT) 2001-2004. FIGT is a globally recognized nonprofit educational organization that focuses on the most critical issues associated with international cultural transitions, www.figt.org.

Beverly believes that relocating families need an information base that allows them to make reasonable relocation decisions. Enabling individuals to have the necessary tools to successfully relocate their families will have a positive impact and reduce costly relocation failures.

# BOOKS IN PRINT

BR Anchor Publishing's books focus on the entire family, providing cost-effective and practical relocation information. Consider a custom book for your company or organization. Visit www.branchor.com/custombooks.htm to preview pages from several of our custom books.

**Books for children:** All three are approved for international and domestic moving. Each contains age-appropriate activities, Internet sites and safety tips. All books are designed to help children to think positively about the transition and turn it into an exciting adventure.

*My Family is Moving* for children 5-8 includes fun moving day countdown calendar stickers and colorful packing labels for children to mark their special belongings. Story characters Oliver Owl and Tommy Turtle prepare youngsters to move to a new home.

*The League of Super Movers* for 9-12 year olds emphasizes that change can bring unexpected benefits. "The League" is a group of superheroes that guides this adventuresome age group through their entire moving adventure.

*Footsteps Around the World* is a one-of-a-kind book that covers everything teens need— from pre-departure planning to how to adjust smoothly to a new location. The many tips include money management, interviews, part-time jobs, talking to parents/teachers and repatriation.

**Books for adults:** *Relocation 101* and *Home Away From Home* provide personal and professional advice for today's most critical relocation challenges. Both books have over 60 Internet sites, relocation checklists and military-specific sections. The wide array of topics include: spouse career options; educational resources; home sales/purchases; medical and elder care and insurance.

*Relocation 101* (domestic) is for individuals moving in and around their own country. It is also appropriate for inpatriates to become oriented to America.

*Home Away From Home* (international) is for families moving to another country. It includes customs and manners and a new section for families moving abroad with infants.

# CONTACT INFORMATION/ORDERS

## BR Anchor Publishing

4596 Capital Dome Drive, Jacksonville, FL 32246-7457
Telephone in the United States 1.800.735.9209
Worldwide telephone: + 904.641.1140,
Facsimile: + 904.641.1136

Amy L. Roman, Publisher: aroman@branchor.com
Beverly D. Roman, Author/Consultant: broman@branchor.com

**ORDERS:** Secure online ordering, V/MC and AMEX accepted
Active government registration

**COMPANY BROCHURE:** Description of company products and services, available at www.branchor.com or email aroman@branchor.com

**CUSTOM BOOKS:** A BR Anchor Publishing Specialty!

## MY INFORMATION

Name _____

Company _____

Address _____

_____

Postal code _____ Country _____

Tel _____ Fax _____

E-mail _____

## www.branchor.com

Visit our website for a wealth of up-to-date relocation information. You will find book excerpts and reviews, custom books and relocation tips. This user-friendly site also offers specialty pages for relocating spouses and employees, an international culture quiz, a secure ordering form and a secure Chat Room to communicate with friends and family around the world.

# NOTES

# NOTES